Discovery of Grace

Discovery of Grace

The birth of God in the soul

Luke Bell

Kevin
Mayhew

First published in 1995 by
KEVIN MAYHEW LTD
Rattlesden
Bury St Edmunds
Suffolk IP30 0SZ

ISBN 0 86209 592 1
Catalogue No 1500017

Front cover: Photography by G. Chapman
Cover design by Graham Johnstone

Typesetting and Page Creation by Vicky Brown
Printed in Hong Kong by Colorcraft Ltd.

For the monks of Quarr Abbey

CONTENTS

PREFACE   9

CHAPTER ONE: RAISING THE WRECK   13
The kingdom of heaven is like a merchant in search of fine pearls, who on finding one pearl of great value went and sold all that he had and bought it. Matthew 13:45-46

CHAPTER TWO: SEEKING AND FINDING   22
Seek, and you will find. Luke 11:9

CHAPTER THREE: THE MASTER   31
'We have found the Messiah.' John 1:41

CHAPTER FOUR: A LIFE BEYOND   40
Blessed are those who mourn, for they shall be comforted. Matthew 5:4

CHAPTER FIVE: NAKEDNESS OF SPIRIT   50
Blessed are the poor in spirit, for theirs is the kingdom of heaven. Matthew 5:3

CHAPTER SIX: WILDEST OF FREEDOMS   60
For if we have been united with him in a death like his, we shall certainly be united with him in a resurrection like his. Romans 6:5

CHAPTER SEVEN: BEYOND SELF   70
Jesus is Lord. 1 Corinthians 12:3

CHAPTER EIGHT: COMMUNION WITH ALL   80
As you did it to one of the least of these my brethren, you did it to me. Matthew 25:40

CHAPTER NINE: THE PERSONAL ARCHETYPE   90
Let it be to me according to your word. Luke 1:38

CHAPTER TEN: MOMENT OF BIRTH   99
And the word became flesh. John 1:14

CHAPTER ELEVEN: DANCING BEYOND TIME   109
When we cry, 'Abba! Father!' it is the Spirit himself bearing witness with our spirit that we are children of God. Romans 8:15-16

CHAPTER TWELVE: THE WATCHING FLOTILLA   119
I will give him a white stone with a new name written on the stone. Revelation 2:17

NOTES   130

ACKNOWLEDGEMENTS   140

PREFACE

The theme of this book is the Christian spiritual path. It is presented in the conviction that the greatness of the gain from the journey along this path is of a different order from any other gain, that it is a gain that transcends limitations of time and space in a way that the finest technology is powerless to do, and that it is a gain not merely for the individual but for the whole world. I hope to persuade my readers that it is a real human possibility and that it is worth all that we have and are. It is possible to fall in love in a matter of minutes in a way that will have a lifetime of consequences. Simply to see the desirability of what has been variously described as sanctity, beatitude, the vision of peace, the celestial city, paradise, is to be ready to begin the journey that costs everything that we think we have and gives us more than we can imagine having. Much has been said and written about this journey in the past. This book aims to show that it does not only belong to the past but can be undertaken now by anyone who really wants to undertake it. It aims to help the reader to see beyond what may appear to be obstacles to the journey and to map it in a way that is not a reflection of an outworn way of thinking but rather an invitation to a way of living so vital that, like the poet John Donne addressing his mistress on the subject of their love, one wonders what one did before.[1]

In writing on this subject, I make no claim for myself other than this: like countless others, I have recognised the authenticity of Christ's teaching through the power of the Holy Spirit. This recognition, and an intuition of the awesome extent of human possibility, has drawn me to reflect on the insights of those who have followed this path. I share my reflections because I think that such sharing can give mutual encouragement. They are addressed not just to the devout but to all who have even the slightest intuition that life might have a meaning. They try to take account of the particular questions that arise about undertaking such a journey in the current climate of thought. The main method of presentation is the use of metaphors. Jesus taught in parables, and this sort of teaching is more apt to awaken the heart to truth than more abstract considerations. However, the metaphors – particularly the one that gives the first chapter its title – are not to be pushed further than they are helpful. Even the gospel teaching can be clouded by a focus on the literal detail: I remember as a young schoolboy being set a particularly frustrating religious education homework that required the manufacture of a lamp such as a wise virgin might have carried.

The first chapter presents and discusses a metaphor that focuses on the work that we do to reach the point of full consent to God's life within us. God chooses to humble himself and wait upon our response to his presence, in order that our response should be free and not coerced. The initiative is in fact always with God in his generous giving of himself, but the metaphor considers the relationship that he begins from our side because this is what *we* can alter. Almost any way of talking about what the metaphor represents is metaphorical: reaching a goal, the birth of God in the soul, and so on. The important thing is not which metaphor we use, but that, like a duckling bonding with its mother, we yoke our deepest yearning to its true destiny. That yearning tends to express itself as a search: this is the theme of the second chapter. The third chapter examines how it is possible for that search to issue in a finding and a commitment – to Christ – without losing any of its openness. The next two chapters consider

Christ's teaching in the beatitudes and in the crucifixion. Chapter Six looks at the freedom that comes from fidelity to this teaching. The following two chapters reflect on how this freedom breaks down the barriers that separate oneself from others. The ninth chapter ponders the complete openness to God that results and its exemplification in Mary, mother of God. Chapter Ten is about the birth of God in our souls. He is always present there, but not always visibly incarnate in our lives. The moment of birth is a spiritual awakening, the goal of the journey, a moment of realisation heralded by the title of this book. The final two chapters look at this new life, born of God, enjoying a transcendent joy, and having an influence and communicating itself beyond all natural limits.

I am grateful to my editor, Michael Forster, for support and help with clarifying the text. I am also grateful to Dr Philip Holt and several of my monastic brethren for their helpful comments on the first draft.

LUKE BELL

＊

CHAPTER ONE

RAISING THE WRECK

*The kingdom of heaven is like a merchant in search of fine
pearls, who on finding one pearl of great value, went and
sold all that he had and bought it.* Matthew 13:45-46

The moment is captured on film. The seeming
impossibility is achieved. From the waters of the Solent
emerge the timbers of a ship sunk more than four
hundred years earlier. The *Mary Rose*, King Henry VIII's
noblest ship of sail, is recovered from the deep and from
the silt. This moment, when the fruit of so much
searching and working is realised, can be seen as a
metaphor for the birth of God in the soul, the moment
when a person can say with St Paul, 'it is no longer I who
live, but Christ who lives in me'.[1] It is the moment when
a person becomes, as Pope Pius XI said of St Thérèse of
Lisieux at her beatification, the word of God for our age.
It is the finding of the Holy Grail, the realisation of
spiritual destiny, the infinite breaking into life and
activity in a human person. This is what Malcolm
Muggeridge is claiming has happened when he writes of
Mother Teresa that 'in a dark time she is a burning and a
shining light; in a cruel time, a living embodiment of
Christ's gospel of love; in a godless time, the Word
dwelling among us, full of grace and truth'.[2] This
becoming is the goal of faith, the greatest gift: God
himself, alive in a person.

The raising of the *Mary Rose* reflects this becoming, this
spiritual realisation. The ship was raised after a long
process demanding vision, courage, determination and
the willingness to be committed to what to many seemed
impossible. In the same way, the spiritual life does not
normally yield its fruit immediately. The growth that

produces it may be over years, over decades or even over a lifetime. It starts too with a search, just as those salvaging the *Mary Rose* had first to locate her.

The first stage of that search is to stop looking in the wrong place. God is not a part of his creation, waiting to be acquired and possessed, as St Augustine realised when he wrote, 'I asked the earth and it said "I am not he";[3] and whatever was in it declared the same'. No amount of terrestrial acquisition can replace God: he is of a different order of being. St Augustine moves towards an understanding of this order of being by comparing the body with the soul that gives it life (something no body can do) and identifies God as the giver of life to the soul which gives life to the body.[4] It follows from this that we are not fully alive if we are not in touch with the source of our life, who is God. Another way of putting it is to say that God is the ground of our being. The implication is that God is within our most vital self: not in our passing feelings or superficial preoccupations. He is the hidden treasure, the paradise within. St Teresa of Avila expressed this in terms of a series of mansions, each hidden within its predecessor like Russian dolls: the goal of the journey (sanctuary and sanctity) is within the innermost mansion. God is to be found in the depth of our own being, as the *Mary Rose* was found in the deep of the sea. To discover him is in some sense to discover our own self, the self of which it can be said:

> This above all: to thine own self be true,
> And it must follow, as the night the day,
> Thou canst not then be false to any man.[5]

The soundings that were taken in the Solent by the archaeologists to locate the ship on the seabed are like the first reaching out by prayer to make contact with God, with our true life. He is always there deep within our soul – indeed he is, as Augustine said, the source of our soul's life – but we are not always in touch with our own depths. The soundings of prayer are a turning in the right direction, away from a preoccupation (which is not the same as involvement) with the outer world, towards inner, spiritual reality. Just as those looking for the *Mary Rose* used what they knew from the past to guide them about where they should make their soundings, so someone beginning their spiritual quest will use, in one way or another, what has been handed on through the ages as a guide as to how to reach towards God. This may simply be the notion that God exists, it may be a set form of prayer, such as the 'Our Father', or it may be a whole network of doctrine and practice learnt from parents and teachers. What matters, since in a sense (like a genetically coded cell) each part contains the whole, is the sincerity of the desire to reach towards God. When we look at our mail in the morning we are naturally more drawn towards those letters that are from someone who really wants to say something to us than to those produced by someone working for a company, for a commercial purpose that means little or nothing to them personally. So the sincere prayer that is as it were the merest scratchings of a pencil will draw God more than the finest piece of desk-top publishing that is an anonymous part of office routine.

A sincere prayer draws God and there results a moment of rapport: a sense of his presence, his love or simply the worthwhileness of continuing a spiritual quest. Now the diving begins. The successful sounding gives the point from which to start. What has been handed on gives necessary parameters so that the diving is not a futile drift from the co-ordinates of the sounding. The diving takes the quester into his or her inner self in the direction of God within. The ocean is an apt symbol for the medium of the journey since its expanse is a natural reflection of eternity. There is an old Arab proverb to the effect that looking at the sea is as good as praying. The nearer we are to God the nearer we are to the limitless possibility that the sea's multidirectional expanse reflects. The word 'recollected', used to designate a prayerful state, describes the condition of the diver: we have recollected where our life has its source, we have remembered about God. The diver is becoming more contemplative, more apt – because more drawn – to turn towards God within, even when the murkiness of the water denies lucid vision. We know that God is there, that our true self is not lost, even when dark or distressing feelings cloud our awareness of it.

However, we do not have a reliable instinct for acting from this self before it is found and uncovered: it is as though, like the timbers of the old ship, it is silted up. Those working on the recovery of the sunken ship had both to find it and to work patiently on the uncovering of the timbers before they could think of raising it. So we have both to find the transcendent beauty that gives life to our souls, and to clean gently away what obscures it. I say 'gently' not simply because the archaeologists excavating the *Mary Rose* in fact used brushes to clean away the silt, but because it is important that the discipline, or ascesis, that this process represents in the spiritual life is not so harsh as to damage morale. As St Benedict says in his rule, the rust must be removed without the pot being broken.[6] It is better to be thinking about the surpassing value of what is to be uncovered than the hatefulness of what is covering it. Indeed – to vary the marine metaphor a little – the psalmist says that God made the monsters of the deep to *play* with. This suggests that the darker aspects of ourselves have the potential of reflecting the divine glory. Any turning inwards may reveal aspects of oneself that seem monstrous, but (like the beasts around the manger) they are to be tamed for God's good pleasure. They are there for him to play with, in the sense of being a source of joy to him. The important thing is to focus on the goal and its great worth, so that energies and aspects of oneself that are not at first part of the mission team are drawn into it, instead of locking in a struggle that distracts from the mission those that are. It is a pearl of great price that we are in the business of buying.[7] Each redirected energy is a jewel from the treasury of the human soul whose value is being reinvested in the greatest of treasures. St John of the Cross said 'One thought alone of man is worth more than the entire world, hence God alone is worthy of it',[8] pointing to the preciousness of the spiritual currency we have to trade with, the talent we have to invest.[9]

The parable of the merchant in search of fine pearls gives us these two co-ordinates for our quest for the birth of God in our soul: the surpassing value of the pearl of great price that we are in quest of and also, by the very fact that they can be exchanged for it, the value of the treasures that we possess. Another way of putting this is to say that God is the supreme good and God loves us. The latter fact gives us our treasure to trade with. It is the reason why one thought alone of ours is worth more than the entire world. How this is so becomes clear if we think about how we react to a child or somebody that we particularly love. A single candid, open, interested, trusting and loving look from such a person can mean more than any amount of things bought or made for us. If the latter does mean as much, it does so in virtue of its indirect expression of what the look expresses directly. If we love, or at the least are open to the possibility of love, then the look is a gift of high value for us. God is love – one more open to love than him cannot be imagined – and therefore 'one thought alone' of him, a single animadversion towards him, a single such look towards him is a gift of high value for *him* and by virtue of being such for him is of high value in itself and absolutely, since he is the source of all value, meaning and indeed being. So it is worth more than the entire world. This is far from surprising in view of the fact that a whole life so oriented can bring to birth the *maker* of the world in the soul. The soul who loses her life (orients it to God, not the world), finds it (gives birth to the maker of the world in herself).[10]

These two co-ordinates give a perspective not only on our spiritual journey, but also on our failures in our journey. The essence of sin is under-selling ourselves in a belittling way. For example, if we respond to another person's weakness by laughing contemptuously instead of giving encouragement, we accept the very limited good of being entertained (in a way that makes us narrower) in place of the greater good of being a nurturer of life (in a way that enlarges our heart and soul). We make a very bad deal. Our thoughts, affections and energies are a currency with a high value: with them we can buy into the currency of the kingdom of heaven (the real gold-standard), we can trade with a view to the purchase of the pearl of great price, the birth of God in our soul. To spend such currency on cheap thrills is a terrible loss. However, for the same reason, it is also misguided to spend the currency of thoughts, affections and energies by dwelling on their earlier misspending. This is to throw good money after bad. That is why Walter Hilton, in the medieval classic description of the spiritual journey, *The Scale of Perfection*, says that a person setting out for Jerusalem (as he puts it) should, once having made a confession of past sins, give them no more attention. It is necessary to acknowledge where we have been misinvesting in order to re-order our foreign currency portfolio, but having done this, to waste opportunities that could be spent in maximising our investment by going over old, infertile ground, is in itself a misinvestment. Every thought of ours is worth more than the entire world. To quote two poets out of context, having acknowledged 'Th'expense of spirit in a waste of shame', we can resolve 'from this night/Not a whisper, not a thought,/Not a kiss nor look be lost.'[11] We are living in the night since we cannot see God face-to-face, but even the smallest signs of love that we can give him have an eternal preciousness.

The metaphor of raising the wreck is only an echo of the oldest and greatest love story, variously told as a quest – for one's true self, for the pearl of great price, for the holy grail, for the philosopher's stone (that is, the stone that turns every suffering and action into the pure gold of love for God) – or as a journey – to one's true home, to the city of peace, to the heavenly Jerusalem. It is meant to be everyone's story, but most of all it is the story of the girl who trustingly and lovingly said 'Behold, I am the handmaid of the Lord; let it be to me according to your word'[12] and, conceiving of the Holy Spirit, gave birth to the Son of God. She models for us a trust and love that can bring God to birth in our own soul, so that he may be incarnate in our life. Trust and love empower God to give himself totally to us, just as we can give of our best when we are trusted and loved and just as a child grows into an adult through being trusted and loved. Of course the power belongs to God, but in his generosity he waits for our invitation to use it, for us to open the door of our lives to him. Mary invited him in trust and love to use his power as he wished.

In making her story our story, and making her trust and love our own, we are accepting as valid what has been passed onto us by others. Each time a person reaches spiritual realisation by following the Christian spiritual path, the truth of this path is accepted and affirmed anew. Affirming it involves a personal recovery of its truth – a recovery for which the raising of the *Mary Rose* can also, in a subordinate sense, serve as a metaphor. This is true even for someone who has grown up with it: unless they are living it for themselves, and not simply as a compliant echo, the commitment needed for perseverance will be absent. It is worth remembering this at the present time when – judging from outward appearances – the Christian tradition itself may appear to be a wreck. It has always been the case that its truth needed to be personally recovered: not indeed for lip-service and attendance at church, but for the courage, never universal, to prefer the things that are unseen and never pass away to the things that are seen and do pass away, even when this preference is won at the cost of life itself.[13] The followers of Christ have always been a sign of contradiction, acting from a motivation radically different from what passes for a norm. What perhaps is different today is the speed with which a mere compliant echo will die away, the impossibility of long maintaining half a commitment or a commitment to the appearance only.

It follows from this that the pioneering quality of each individual journey in faith is now more apparent. Just as it required vision and determination to recover the *Mary Rose*, so, more apparently than before, does the recovery of the life-giving truths of our spiritual tradition require vision and determination. But the very isolation of the person setting out to do this is a measure of the depth and prevalence of the need for this recovery. The attention that Mother Teresa receives is an indication of this need. It has in reality always been with us: for example, each of St Benedict, St Francis and St Teresa of Avila recovered these truths at a time when civilisation itself seemed to hang on such a recovery. As for the apparently wrecked nature of the Christian tradition: St Peter's triple denial must have looked wrecking, as have later schism, controversy and defection; as did the crucifixion of Christ. And yet the gates of hell have not prevailed and will not prevail.[14] Even if a mother turns away the child at her breast, God will not turn from the one who seeks him.[15]

The search, the recovery, the raising of the wreck has a multiple aspect. We have touched upon both the initial personal rediscovery of the truth of the Christian spiritual tradition and on its final fruition in the birth of God in the soul. These will both be explored more fully in the pages that follow, but we shall also be concerned with the correction of perspective on our own age. This is the recovery of vision that facilitates personal rediscovery of spiritual truth and the birth of God in the soul, and the many recoveries to be accomplished on the journey from the former to the latter: recovery of a teacher, of life, of orientation of heart, of freedom, of one's true self, of community. The first movement of this journey is this personal rediscovery of the truth – the step into the life of faith. For one hesitating before taking this step, it may well seem that all these nautical metaphors are inappropriate. If God is within, he does not appear to be within reach of a diving expedition. Rather he is buried beyond ken in hard frosty soil whose flints mock the digger for treasure. The next chapter looks at this step of the pilgrimage.

CHAPTER TWO

SEEKING AND FINDING

Seek, and you will find. Luke 11:9

The person seeking God is already on the pilgrimage to him, even if the seeking appears to be no more than the futile clanging of a spade against stones. If the tenderness of God is locked within the hard crust of the earthly self, the spirit of God is inspiring the search for him. It is part of the generosity of God that it may seem to us that we are doing the searching: we are being weaned from our self-centredness to a realisation of our total dependence on him gradually, in the measure that we can take it. So there is a sense in which

> . . . the end of all our exploring
> Will be to arrive where we started
> And know the place for the first time.[1]

It is a waking up to reality: the reality that it is God and not our superficial self who is at the centre of everything, and that God is searching, is longing for our freely given love with a tenderness and love that surpasses all that we can imagine. Not long ago I dreamt that I was going from place to place seeking a bed to sleep in. I woke from this dream in a warm, comfortable bed. This is the condition of imperfect faith: to dream that one is in search of something of whose possession waking will give the assurance.

The firstlings of faith can predate any direct thought of God himself. There is a basic urge to meaning in every person which is the seed of faith. This can be variously expressed. Simply acting on the feeling that it is worth getting out of bed in the morning shows a certain commitment to finding life meaningful. When a child asks questions, there is behind them a conviction that there is a meaning to be found. The raw expectation that life is going to mean something is to a fully formed faith what the gurgling of a baby is to articulate speech. If we consider how pleasing this baby's gurgling is to its parents, we can get an idea of God's perspective on our urge to meaning. An inchoate intuition that everything does somehow make sense, in an albeit yet unperceived way, means more to God our loving Father than any amount of heartless parroting of the creed, just as the baby's first essay in communication means more to its parents than would cold and insincere formalities from grown-up children. Even the parents, let alone God to whom a thousand years is as a day, can see that there is a promise of growth in the first beginnings. But if there is no growth in communication – if the mental limitations of the child preclude the emergence of articulate speech[2] – who shall say that the parents may not have a special tenderness for this child? Who shall legislate as to what is a saving faith? Perhaps some such thought is behind the inclusion in the fourth eucharistic prayer of the Catholic Church of an intercession 'for all the dead whose faith is known to you alone', shortly after one for 'all who seek you with a sincere heart'. What matters is that faith, even if it is in its most embryonic form, is alive. Bodily death does not kill it. It can only be killed by absolute wilful despair or by absolute pride. Although these show themselves in different ways, at their most extreme they converge, since the extreme of pride is the refusal to contemplate any good beyond the narrowly egotistic self and therefore, like the extreme of wilful despair, the refusal to reach out to it. Faith reaches out to the good (to God) beyond our egotistic self, or, to put it in a way that is consonant with the metaphors that we have been using, reaches within to allow God to emerge from the hard shell of the egotistic self.

The urge to meaning (the seed of faith) is evident in the very use of language. This presupposes the existence of meaning and therefore is a kind of inchoate faith.[3] Of course it is possible to speak with hardly any meaning, indeed to use language as a barrier to stop the truth breaking in. People do this, for example, when they do not want to come to terms with a strong feeling, or when they fear that a pause will give another person a chance to say something that they would rather not hear. The observation of this use of language points to a truth about the urge to meaning which is true of its manifestations in language, music and articulated faith. It needs silence. Silence is to spoken language what God within is to the human person. The less awareness there is of its presence, the more language tends to the superficial and lacking in meaning. In the same way the more a person is without awareness of the presence of God within them (whether or not this presence is articulated as such), the more their living tends to the superficial and the lacking in profound purpose. The importance of silence for language is reflected in the use of pauses in the art of public speaking. The importance of the awareness of the presence of God within for the human person is reflected in the practice of going on retreat in the art of the spiritual life. Silence is needed for meaning. It is also needed for becoming aware of the presence of God, who is the source of all meaning. Silence is both the space within language where its meaning nestles and also the space within the articulations of faith where God dwells. The direction of the pilgrimage towards God is a move towards an inner silence.

The belief in meaning inherent in language (as well as in simply getting on with life) bears witness to the human tendency towards faith, which is the ability to respond to the signposts (the doctrines of faith) on the journey towards the silent, all-giving mystery. There are other witnesses to this urge to meaning. Literature, which is the unclumsy use of language, articulates a sense of meaning in life. Literature awakens the reader to the symbolic power of the natural world: a sunset speaks of, in some sense means, mortality; mercy 'droppeth as the gentle rain from heaven'.[4] Literature sees a meaning and harmony which is both within and beyond our life and creates an image of its integrity. Psychology too bears witness to the human urge to meaning, a theme particularly explored by Victor Frankl in his book *Man's Search for Meaning*, which testifies to its importance when a person is faced with extraordinary trials.[5] These ways in which people reach out for meaning point to the existence of ultimate meaning. The Christian faith teaches that this is the *Logos*, the Word of God made flesh.

In one sense this ultimate meaning is obvious, in the etymological sense of this word, of being right in our path. The body of Christ is manifested at the consecration in the eucharist and the Church herself – all those who receive the body of Christ in communion – is the body of Christ. However, to the person on the journey towards faith it may not be so obvious. Searching the stony soil of the soul for a place where the mustard seed of faith can germinate, they may ask

> What are the roots that clutch, what branches grow
> Out of this stony rubbish?[6]

The quotation is taken from T. S. Eliot's poem *The Wasteland*, which presents an image of a culture in which a participant 'can connect/Nothing with nothing'.[7] This poem suggests that we are living in a time when the urge to meaning is being frustrated in an unprecedented way. So does much else: such as, for example, literary theories that attack the idea that literature has a communicable meaning, and people taking their own lives. It seems that though the objects of faith in ultimate meaning (Christ, his Church and sacraments) may be obvious, the faith itself is not obvious in the sense of being there, immediately available to satisfy the urge to meaning. If it were, unbelievers would be unusual in our society. So it is worth asking, as part of our examination of the path towards the birth of God in the soul, what obstacles are placed on the initial stretch of that path by the spirit of this age and what sort of perspective on them can aid progress.

When we are in the pursuit of truth it is important for us to be alert to prejudices so that we can avoid the danger of our thinking being distorted by them. In certain ways the spirit of the present age is very aware of possible prejudices. For example, no one who dismissed St Augustine's teaching on the grounds that he came from Africa and was therefore black would get much of a hearing. Anyone who tried to disparage the sublime wisdom of St Teresa of Avila on the grounds that this great doctor of the Church is a woman would soon be told where they had gone wrong. People can see the pride, and therefore error, in racism and sexism. If someone says, 'You have to be white, and a man like me before I will take your thinking seriously,' it will not go unnoticed how self-centredness is cutting that person off from truth. However, there is one prejudice that is so generally unperceived as not to rank as a prejudice at all in common estimation. This is the prejudice that our own age is wiser than those that have gone before it. I call this epochism. St Augustine and St Teresa can get past the barriers of racism and sexism and be stopped in their tracks by epochism.

Epochism distorts the thinking of the present age in the same way that self-centredness can distort the thinking of an individual. A self-centred individual will tend to overrate the importance of the contribution he has to make. There is a wonderful example of this in the film *The Dresser*, where the actor-manager of a theatre company touring during the war presents a couple of free tickets for his play to a man whose house has just been destroyed in a bombing raid, and cannot understand why he is not consoled. Similarly, a self-centred person who has specialised in a particular area of thinking will tend to assume that everything that matters is properly dealt with by this sort of expertise. For example, it might not occur to a self-centred financial expert that the best their competence could offer somebody could still leave them unhappy. In the same way, this age tends to assume that its particular expertise is applicable to everything.

The particular expertise of this age is in the natural, or material sciences. It is competent to deal with material things. Therefore, on this level – having flush toilets and being able to get to places quickly, for example – we are well provided for. The distortion in thinking comes when an attempt is made to view the human and, even more so, the divine within the boundaries of this limited competence. We can see how this goes wrong if we reflect on how well a person would get to know us who treated us as though we were a thing. If our thoughts were to be reduced to being no more than the weight of our brain and our feelings no more than the chemistry of our blood, the observer of these data would not know us at all. Indeed, we would feel affronted by anyone claiming really to know us in this way. This feeling gives an indication of what is wrong with this way of trying to know people. It does not show enough respect. It treats a person as though they were not an equal to the observer – an equivalent centre of consciousness – but as though they were below the observer, rightly to be mastered in the way a material thing might be. If this methodology is wrong for examining another person who deserves an equal respect to oneself, it is even more disastrously wrong for thinking about God, who deserves a greater respect than oneself. As Shakespeare said, 'Take but degree away, untune that string,/And hark what discord follows'.[8] It is the discord of atheism. The atheistic tendency in the present age is due to the fact that the personal and the divine are approached with the cast of thought that is only appropriate for dealing with the material. We can only really know another person, really receive their unfolding life, if we love and trust them. In our self-giving is our communion and so our knowledge. So it is with God: in our love and trust of Him and our giving of ourselves to Him, we come to know Him.

The digger searching for God needs not a degree in earth sciences but to listen to the parable:

> The kingdom of heaven is like treasure hidden
> in a field, which a man found and covered up;
> then in his joy he goes and sells all he has and
> buys that field.[9]

All that he has, his full self, needs to be brought to the search for God. The intuition, the first inkling of ultimate meaning needs to be protected from loss ('covered up') while a joyful self-giving wins the ultimate prize. In looking for the field with the treasure hidden in it, it makes sense to consider reports from the past. Perhaps a map from a former time can show the exact spot where the treasure is buried. The great Doctors of the Church and guides to the spiritual life (Saints Teresa & Augustine, for example) can help us find the spiritual treasure we seek, if we can overcome the epochist prejudice that their testimony is to be looked down on because it does not belong to our age. Indeed, part of the quest is recovering the wisdom of the past. Nobody looking for the *Mary Rose* would have said, 'This chart (showing where she is) is no use, it's not the latest thing!'

Yet the epochism of the age tends to blind it to the fact that what it is good at is not the right way of knowing God. The tender love of St Teresa of Avila, which has found God, is denied validity because it is too great to be known by a methodology that, essentially, looks down on it. This is to trade one's birthright (divine life) for a mess of pottage (domination of the material world).[10] But what shall it profit a man if he gains the entire world, but loses his immortal soul?[11] Why pretend that what we have more readily available, mastery of the material, is the proper measure of all that there is, for the sake of the superficial easiness of feeling good and walking tall?

We need to avoid a pride in this epoch that blinds us to what the great souls of the past have to tell us. It is equally important, however, to see why we should not despair of it – it may be in reality that this is the greater danger. So we should also consider the hopeful aspects of our own age. Firstly, there is, as there always has been, as with Noah, as with Abraham, as with the Israelites, a faithful remnant of the people of God. As long as there is one Carthusian monk or one Carmelite nun living for the love of God, the world is graced and the city of our civilisation is marked against destruction. Secondly – and those of us who live by the values of the faithful remnant need to remember this as a corrective to personal pride – there is hope of salvation in any honest search for truth. The transcendent cannot be excluded from profound researches. So, there are scientists whose thinking leads them towards seeing the impossibility of a total theory of the universe, explaining it in terms of itself alone.[12] In a similar way, those reflecting on the meaning of art and culture, such as George Steiner in his book, *Real Presences*,[13] are, by following contemporary thinking to its logical conclusion, seeing that meaning and communication are finally dependent on divine authority. The absurdity of a relativism that postulates the absence of the absolute as an absolute is becoming more and more apparent. Thinking faithfully is taking people back to the truth. Thirdly, and most importantly, there is the justice of God. Because of the justice of God, the greater the difficulty of belief (because of circumstances such as widespread contemporary error), the greater the abundance of grace for those who wish to step towards the truth. For this reason, this is an age of exceptional spiritual opportunity. It is almost as if God, in His fathomless humility, were as one of us might be at a time when we were generally unpopular and shunned – heart-winningly grateful for the least interest and kindness. We can be sure that he will not be outdone in generosity.

Part of that generosity, as the beginning of this chapter suggested, is his presence hidden within our search. It is the Holy Spirit within who inspires and guides us in our seeking. If the doctrines and sacraments of the Christian faith are the objective pole of God's revelation, the Holy Spirit within our hearts is its subjective pole. What is divine outside one's heart says the same thing as what is divine within one's heart. This accounts for the sense of homecoming people feel in taking a step forward in faith.[14] It is as though they have half a sixpence and they are being offered another half-sixpence that exactly matches it, like one who has made a love-tryst by breaking the coin in two.[15] It is a poignant moment in a story of love.

THE MASTER

'We have found the Messiah'. John 1:41

'No one can say "Jesus is Lord" except by the Holy Spirit.'[1] It is God the Holy Spirit within us who recognizes God the Son. This loving matching of half-sixpences is the core of revelation. St Paul's description of the divinely inspired recognition of the divine reflects the experience of his co-propagator of the Christian revelation, St Peter, as it is described in St Matthew's gospel:

> He said to them, 'But who do you say that I am?' Simon Peter replied, 'You are the Christ, the Son of the living God.' And Jesus answered him, 'Blessed are you, Simon Bar-Jona! For flesh and blood has not revealed this to you, but my Father who is in heaven.'[2]

God – not flesh and blood – reveals God to Peter. In this revelation of God by God to a man is the genesis of the Christian Church.[3] Each member of this church is such by the same process, through being able to say, 'Jesus is Lord' by the Holy Spirit. The inner pole of revelation corresponds to the outer pole of revelation, the substance of the human spirit welcomes the gift of the manifestation of its eternal home.

When, as it is related in St John's gospel, Andrew said to his brother, 'We have found the Messiah', he was talking about the fulfilment of an expectation that a whole people had cherished in their hearts for generation after generation. The contemporary digger for truth who is finding the ground stony does not necessarily expect that a single person will be 'the way, and the truth and the life'.[4] It is worth asking therefore what initial stages of reflection can prepare for this moment of finding and recognition. Another way of putting the question (bearing in mind what was said in the previous chapter about epochism) is to ask what might have been lost that would facilitate such a recognition. Part of an answer to this question might be that in the current climate of thought the special dignity in the creation of the human person has been partially lost to sight.

The saying of St John of the Cross quoted in Chapter One, 'one thought alone of man is worth more than the entire world', articulates the perspective that has tended to fade from view. This has happened because of a tendency to overvalue the exterior at the expense of the interior. If we consider a person only from an exterior point of view they may appear insignificant in comparison with the vast expanses of the creation. If on the other hand we consider the value of human thought, as indicated by St John of the Cross, then the relative smallness of the space occupied by a person appears insignificant. A qualitative difference in the human person – an ability to know and love and hence to reach out to God who transcends all creation – makes them much more important than any amount of mere physical expanse. This is obvious to any parent or lover, who would not exchange the child or beloved who knows and loves them for all the tea in China.

A crisis of confidence comes, however, once people lose a sense of the value of their own ability to know and love, through which they recognize the value of the other person. To lose this is to under-sell oneself, to forget that any amount of exterior things cannot make up for this ability: what shall it profit a man if he gains the entire world and lose his immortal soul?[5] This under-selling of oneself, trading the spiritual for the material, is only possible if we forget that we are able to know and love the creator of the entire world. If we remember that we are made by him, for him and in his image, then we can see that we share his transcendence of the world. Each person in some sense includes the whole world in themself, by being able to apprehend it.[6] However, each person is also destined for God who transcends the world, since they have a heart which even all the world cannot satisfy.

In the light of this it makes sense to replace the question 'Is the human person at home in the world?' with the statement that the world is at home in the human person and the human person is at home in God. To speak thus is not to condone the perversion of the sense of human transcendence of the world that has led to actions destructive of the environment. This is the work of a humanity not seeking its home in God; the ravages of the dominating, controlling ego being preferred to the birth of God within; the choice of exterior domination over inner surrender to the source of life. It is looking for salvation in what the age is good at (controlling the material) instead of where alone it can be found (in God). The epochist attitude of prioritising the former both devastates the world and leaves humanity feeling homeless. On the other hand, the return to God in humility is also a return to proper self-esteem: by recognising its sublime destiny, humanity loses the need of a restless and destructive insecurity to carve its name on the fabric of creation. It wins instead the 'new name written on the stone which no one knows except him who receives it'.[7]

All this suggests why we should expect to find our way to God through a person, but not why the 'new name'[8] should be bestowed by this particular person who has 'the name which is above every name'. Why should it be God's plan 'to unite all things in him, things in heaven and things on earth'?[9] One of the stones in the digger-for-truth's soil may be the question of why it should be a single person in whom all are truly to find themselves. A hint of an answer might be given by the experience of being in love, where all that matters seems to be in a single person. It should also be said that, as the final two chapters will show, there is no question here of anybody losing their true identity or role because there is another as the leader or teacher: rather it is through his facilitation that each finds their true identity, their 'new name'. This includes working with him to help others receive their 'new name'.

The main part of the answer, however, comes back to the reflections above about expanse and interiority, the material and the spiritual. It only looks as though a person is relatively unimportant compared with the great expanse of material creation if one ignores the quality that the person has that puts them on a different plane, one that includes but also transcends the material. If one person's thought 'is worth more than the entire world' so that their inner world (a microcosm of the creation) has a greater value than the merely earthly world, then why should not one person embrace all persons if he is both human and divine? Just as a person's humanity puts them above the material world while remaining in it and being able to fashion it so that it speaks of the transcendent, so his divinity puts him above the merely human, while still being human and being able to transform human nature so that it is caught up into the divine life.

Just as it only looks as though a person is relatively unimportant compared to the great mass of (for example) a mountain if the judgement is made by merely material standards, so it only looks as though one person cannot be important enough 'to unite all things in himself' if the judgement is made by merely human standards. By the

merely human standards of prestige and power, a death
by crucifixion under the Roman Empire is as low as you
can get. The resurrection tells us that there is a higher,
divine standard. It is because of his very transcendence of
human standards – 'taking the form of a servant' and
becoming 'obedient unto death, even a death on a cross' –
that there is

> bestowed on him the name which is above
> every name, that at the name of Jesus every
> knee should bow, in heaven and on earth, and
> every tongue confess that Jesus Christ is Lord,
> to the glory of God the Father.[10]

This centrality of a single person implies that personal
relations are not ultimately defined in time and space.
This is a theme that will be explored more fully later, but
it will help put our current considerations in perspective
to touch on it here. Moments of real communion between
people are often marked by silence rather than words (or
if words, then words which take their force from silence),
and the deeper the communion the more subtle the
physical movement that articulates it. This implies that,
as with communion with God, silence is of the essence of
interpersonal communion. The possibility of communion
in the absence even of personal presence is suggested by
the description given by Patrick White, in his novel *Voss*,
of a spiritual relationship that ignores the space of the
Australian outback. That personal presence can extend
beyond death as well as space is intimated not only by
the response of saints to intercession, but by the
not uncommon sense of presence of loved ones who
have died.

There are hints too in the structure of physical reality
that distance is not the measure of personal communion.
As well as the technology of telecommunications (which,

to give an old-fashioned example, include your being able to read this book!), there is the way in which, in a growing organism, each cell contains the identity of the whole creature. Although it is not an exact analogy since the identity is in all the cells not just one of them, this hints at the way a single person might contain the essential identity of each human person. Something of the same sort is seen in a brilliant work of art, such as a play by Shakespeare, where a single phrase encapsulates the theme of the whole. For example, the quotation from *Hamlet* in Chapter One[11] gives us the entire drama in miniature. The hologram also suggests how a single identity can be omnipresent and recent work in physics implies that there may be more dimensions than three in space and one in time. Certainly the workaday measurements of space and time do not give us absolute reality. Only God is absolute and God is present in everything sustaining it in being (otherwise it could not exist) and (because God cannot be split up into parts) all of God is present in everything.[12] It is only the perspective of time and space that makes this difficult to conceive. To the visionary, such as William Blake, eternity is to be seen in a grain of sand.

These considerations suggest why it is reasonable for the seeker of truth to turn to the person of Jesus. There may, however, be yet another stone in the soil of our digger. The very idea of finding the truth may suggest a narrowing commitment. There is general acceptance of the value of openness to what is true, but a statement of the sort made by Andrew, 'We have found the Messiah', is regarded with greater suspicion because it is thought to be an exclusion of other possibilities. This suspicion arises because the eternal nature of truth has been lost sight of. To find the Messiah is not to say, 'The search is over now, I can close my mind', but to be truly open to the infinite possibilities of truth because one is in touch with the source of the life of the whole creation. It is to know the life and the light that puts all knowledge in the perspective of eternity so that nothing sublunary is regarded as the last word.[13] It is liberation from a life limited to the patterns of one's own knowledge, a launching into mystery, wonder and gratitude.

To find the Messiah, to follow him, is to be taught by him to abandon what constrains and limits life: he came that we might have life and have it abundantly.[14] His teaching is the subject of the next two chapters, but it is appropriate in this chapter to consider the whole question of teaching authority. In doing this, we are not so much digging for treasure as concerned to make the ground less stony before his seed is scattered on it. Authority has a bad name because of its misuse. However, if it comes from God, the author of all things, it is by definition pure of this corruption. At the end of his great summary of Jesus' teaching St Matthew says, 'The crowds were astonished at his teaching, for he taught them as one who had authority, and not as their scribes'.[15] The question that faces us today is how this teaching can make a similar impact now. Part of the answer is at the beginning of this chapter: the Holy Spirit teaches inwardly what is presented outwardly. Simply to read chapters five, six and seven of St Matthew's Gospel under the guidance of the Spirit is to be open to Jesus' teaching.

The teaching is passed on through scripture, but also through the Church, its tradition and representatives. In each case it is received in the individual person through the inspiration of the Holy Spirit. Through the ages and also today there are many witnesses to the power of this teaching, 'the way' as it was called in its early days.[16] The author of the letter to the Hebrews exhorts us:

> Since we are surrounded by so great a cloud of witnesses, let us also lay aside every weight,

> and sin which clings so closely, and let us run
> with perseverance the race that is set before us,
> looking to Jesus the pioneer and perfecter of our
> faith, who for the joy that was set before him
> endured the cross, despising the shame, and is
> seated at the right hand of the throne of God.[17]

The witnesses he refers to are in fact those from among the
people of Israel who showed faith, but the words apply
equally well to Christians who have shown faith. We can
see in the lives of the saints, who have been transformed
into radiations of God's love, the fruit of the teaching and
saving work of Jesus. It is by this fruit that we know the
authority of the teaching. It works. In assessing the appeal
of the spiritual life it makes sense to look to these
examples, rather than the example of merely nominal
followers, just as, for someone who knew nothing of the
appeal of music, it would make sense to be introduced to
Mozart, rather than the jingle of an ice-cream van. As well
as individual lives we have too the witness of Christian
civilization. The purpose, the cohesion, the traditions of
justice and mercy, the art, the literature and the science of
Christendom are not merely accidental. Without the light
of Christian teaching they would not have come to birth.
Again, it makes sense to judge from the positive
achievement, not the failures: no-one maintains that
everybody has always acted in the light.

The culmination of positive outcomes from the
teaching of Jesus witnesses outwardly what the Holy
Spirit witnesses inwardly: this has divine authority. If we
reflect on the nature of even the most basic aspect of our
civilization, the communication of meaning through
language, we can see that there has to be some sort of
established norm to make it work, lest society break
down in the babble of a million private languages.[18] So
too there is a need for a grammar of growth towards

God: the teaching of Jesus is that grammar. The need for the Messiah's teaching, for ultimate meaning, is such that an absolute quality has been attributed to the teachings of individuals who are not the Son of God. If absolute dogmatism among followers of Marx and Freud is on the decline, it is because they are being known by their fruits.[19]

If there is also a turning away from Christian spiritual teaching and its authority, in the form of an eclectic 'New Age' philosophy that is focused on the worship of the earth, that is an indication of the need for its full recovery. It is said that every heresy is the revenge of a neglected truth. In this case, not only has the true nature of human participation in divine transcendence been lost sight of in godless exploitation of the planet, but also the immanence of God in his creation has been neglected. The answer is to affirm both that God is above humanity and that he is within all that he has created. Both the ideas of beyond and within are needed to express what can be said about the truth of God. If in this book images of within (sea, soil and so on) predominate, that is because it is the comparative neglect of this aspect in recent centuries that has led both to grave misconceptions (such as the idea that God is merely 'out there' and does not care about us) and to the opposite and grave error of, in effect, worshipping the creation instead of the creator. God is both transcendent and immanent, and it is in the coincidence of these opposites (to use the phrase of Nicholas of Cusa) that he is to be found.

This chapter has been concerned with clearing the ground of obstacles to the search for God. The digger of stony ground that we met at the beginning of the last chapter who was inspired by the Spirit without really understanding what was going on – he could see no hope of treasure – may be supposed to have been tilling the soil, by the Spirit's guidance, for the sowing of the divine word. We now turn to listen to that word.

CHAPTER FOUR

A LIFE BEYOND

Blessed are those who mourn, for they shall be comforted.
Matthew 5:4

The beatitudes given in Chapter Five of St Matthew's Gospel are a summary of the teaching of Jesus. They offer the possibility of a life which is not dependent on any earthly contingencies, a blessedness that transcends what the world has to offer. When Jesus says, 'Blessed are those who mourn, for they shall be comforted,' he is pointing to the paradoxical value of loss in the same way as he is when he says, 'Whoever loses his life for my sake, he will save it'.[1] That is not all that this beatitude teaches – it also about the value of facing, accepting and grieving a loss – but this is the essence of the teaching. Beyond the necessary therapeutic process of grieving is the fact of loss: this is the essence of what is blessed. This interpretation is born out by a comparison with St Luke's presentation of the beatitudes. There those that are said to be blessed are '. . . you poor, . . . you that hunger now, . . . you that weep now, . . . you when men hate you, and when they exclude you and revile you'.[2] The fact that this refers to loss of riches, food, merriment and reputation is made clear by what follows: 'Woe to you that are rich, for you have received your consolation', and a similar pronouncement on those who '. . . are full now, . . . that laugh now' and those of whom 'all men speak well'.[3]

The apparent absurdity of the stark paradox 'loss is blessedness' is a challenge to thought. The question is raised of what is so very good that it more than makes up for the loss of all that is normally held to constitute a happy life. How are the poor, hungry, weeping, hated and excluded blessed? The admonition addressed to the rich, 'You have received your consolation', is an implication that there is a consolation for the bereft, and the statement 'Blessed are those that mourn, for they shall be comforted' promises comfort to the grieving. What is it? There is a clue in the saying, 'Whoever loses his life for my sake, he will save it,' and also in the saying, 'The thief comes only to steal and kill and destroy; I came that they may have life and have it abundantly'.[4] It is a special kind of life, the life that is found by losing what is normally considered as life. It is a life that is abundant and invulnerable, not dependent on riches, food, merriment, or reputation. It is a life without 'ifs', a life that does not flourish only if one is rich, well-fed, merry and well spoken of. It is the life of one who is totally and unconditionally alive: sheer life.

The nature of this life becomes clearer if we consider the normal experience of feeling alive.[5] A sense of life, of being alive, is usually felt in connection with a particular situation: for example, having dinner in good company, walking around the battlements of a moon-lit castle with someone with whom we are in love, or winning a game. We feel a sense of life if we are doing this. It is dependent on the particular situation. The life that Jesus proclaims in the beatitudes is not like this. It depends on no particular circumstances: not even money, abundance of food or being liked by people. It swings free of all these things: they are not necessary, considered as lost, Jesus explains, 'for my sake'. These words and those quoted above, 'I came that they might have life and have it abundantly' tell us where the aliveness of the beatitudinal life comes from: Jesus himself. In the ordinary sort of aliveness, the sense of life comes from an aspect of creation (the well-cooked steak, particular company and so on): in this case it comes from him through whom all things were created – the eternal source of life himself.

It is direct, unmediated life. Not only does it have an eternal power that is undiluted by anything created, it cannot – unlike life dependent on a particular situation – be unwillingly lost. St Paul asks, 'Who shall separate us from the love of Christ? Shall tribulation, or distress, or persecution, or famine, or nakedness, or peril, or sword?' and answers his own question:

> No, in all these things we are more than conquerors through him who loved us. For I am sure that neither death, nor life, nor angels, nor principalities, nor things present, nor things to come, nor powers, nor height, nor depth, nor anything else in all creation, will be able to separate us from the love of God in Christ Jesus our Lord.[6]

The blessedness of this life is what the beatitudes proclaim: an undying love that transcends everything. In the light of this, the significance of the loss that the beatitudes pronounce blessed is clear. It is the loss of unhealthy constraint and limitation, of a life squeezed into something too narrow for it, and a concomitant finding of unlimited life. It is not that money, food, human approval and so on are bad. They are not good *enough*. The whole world is not enough to satisfy the human heart. Only God, the source of all life, can do that. Experiences of loss enable us to exchange a partial good for an absolute good, trading in, as it were, a ticket for a single journey for a free pass for the whole travel network.[7]

It is an escape from a limiting addiction, which restlessly seeks joy in something particular that cannot possibly give absolute fulfilment, to a finding of peace and a joy of which it can be said, 'no one will take your joy from you'.[8] This makes it clear why Jesus says 'woe to you who are full now'. It is as though, to compare the ridiculous with the sublime, someone has made such a pig of themself in eating the indifferent *hors d'oeuvre* to a meal that they have no room left for the delicious main course. The comparison only really expresses the point if we think of the main meal as of a completely different order of being from the other food: as different as the creator is from the creation. To reflect on what Jesus offers when he talks of abundant life is to see what is meant by the thief who comes only to steal and kill and destroy. This thief is anybody who, unlike the life-giving saviour, offers a mere imitation of life. It is someone who offers, for example, heroin, loveless sexual gratification or empty flattery as though it fulfilled the deepest longings of the heart. More pernicious, perhaps, because less obviously so and less likely to be fought against, is the offer of public respectability and material comforts in exchange for inalienable and eternal life. Such deals are a swindle from the father of lies. They breed a dependency that inhibits and restricts life; they make happiness conditional on particular outcomes.

Somebody who finds happiness through Jesus, on the other hand, somebody who is 'blessed', has a happiness that is not restricted at all. They are able to respond gratefully to his love, which is the foundation of their happiness, whatever the circumstances. And because Jesus is God he can reciprocate open-heartedness to an infinite degree. The blessedness of the loss celebrated by the beatitudes is that it weans us from the frustrating addiction which seeks happiness in what cannot meet the yearning of the human heart for bliss. This frustration is highlighted by those cases where someone amasses great quantities of a particular limited good (such as a specific kind of material possession, or fame) only to find that mere quantity of this limited good cannot meet the longing of the heart for the absolute. Each additional acquisition fails to bring what is sought, as a bird trapped behind a pane of glass fails with each beat of its wings to free itself. Only Jesus can give absolute love. The walking free from the frustration is a consummation devoutly to be wished. Once achieved, the deepest (immortal) self is free from being damaged by the heart-ache and the thousand natural shocks that flesh is heir to. At the end of the cowboy story *Shane*, Shane rides away. He has done what he has to do and yet he has not become entangled. This is an image of life of the free (that is, Jesus-focused) person.

The death too of a Jesus-focused person is like this. Just as no material or worldly good has an absolute importance, so mortal life itself is not clung to as though it can give what Jesus alone can give. He gives a life that goes beyond death. He is the resurrection and the life, and whoever believes in him 'though he die, yet shall he live'.[9] His resurrection gives life to all of his own. Mother Teresa was once in a situation where her life was threatened. Her response to her threatener was that if she were killed she would be with God sooner. It is a wonderful freedom, this life promised by the beatitudes: nothing, no deprivation, no threat, not death itself can take it away.

It is therefore worth some effort to achieve it. It is reached through prayer, which develops the relationship with the source of absolute life, and through ascesis. Sometimes the latter is called mortification, which has perhaps unfortunate connotations. All it means is the dying of limitation: the limited life needs to be exchanged for unlimited life. Ascesis is also sometimes referred to as spiritual discipline – this is a learning (as a disciple learns) of what makes for unlimited life. Whatever it is called, the essential is the dynamic thrust towards absolute life. This is a good that makes the effort and the trouble of the learning worthwhile. St Benedict (in his rule) encourages those to whom it may seem a strict discipline:

Do not be daunted immediately by fear and run away from the road that leads to salvation. It is bound to be narrow at the outset. But as we progress in this way of life and in faith, we shall run on the path of God's commandments, our hearts overflowing with the inexpressible delight of love.[10]

The submarine work done on the wreck of the *Mary Rose* can, as was suggested in Chapter One, be seen as a metaphor for the efforts made on the way to reaching a point where we are spiritually running with hearts overflowing with the inexpressible delight of love. Each timber cleaned is part of the preparation of the whole ship. Every silted up motive of the heart that is purified by prayer is a preparation for the day when it is ready to overflow. Each uncovering of what has lain under the mud of the deep brings nearer the recovery of the ship. Each hidden energy that is discovered and turned to God is a greater readiness for the day when he is all in all to the soul. Everything is in dynamic tension towards the joy of raising the ship, the joy of the birth of God in the soul. Every mourning of the loss of a limited good is the shadow caused by the bright sun of the comfort of the kingdom. Every leaving is a journey towards God in whom everything is found and found aright.

The work of ascesis or spiritual discipline (preparing the ship to be raised, as it were) can be undertaken in the religious life where a vow of obedience detaches the soul from her wishes for any particular thing so that she is freed to bring her heart to Jesus, the source of everything. However, in every life there is the same basic discipline: the frustrations of everyday living. These can vary from a bus being late to a heart-breaking betrayal. The spiritual principle is the same, nonetheless: each thwarting is an encouragement to be emancipated from an investment in what is limited so as to reinvest in the unlimited. To do so is to be clothed with Christ, who offers boundless life. The thwarted aspects of life, which seem such a solid and necessary expression of it, become the husk of a seed that has to decompose so that the true life of the living plant can emerge – perhaps a tree that can give shelter to many.[11] The final decay of the husk is a release into the greatest possible life: death of the earthly body brings eternal life.

The beatitudes are a chart telling us how to locate the treasure of the sea, the ship of eternal beatitude. Each tells us either what needs to be cleaned away to find it, or where we need to look. 'Blessed are the meek, for they shall inherit the earth'[12]: if we can clean away the false pride that blocks our vision with its selfishly partial perspective, we shall have our eyes opened to unlimited life. This life comes from the creator himself, who holds all of creation in being. It is therefore in touch with his indwelling presence in all creation. The earth itself belongs to those who have this life, because they have penetrated its inner mystery. 'Blessed are those who hunger and thirst for righteousness, for they shall be satisfied'[13]: if we long for what is right, for God's will, we shall be filled with what alone can satisfy – the indwelling presence of God. 'Blessed are the merciful, for they shall obtain mercy'[14]: those who bring God's tenderness to others necessarily enjoy it themselves. The barrier between another's need and one's own heart is the same as the barrier between one's own heart and God. 'Blessed are the pure in heart, for they shall see God'[15]: those who want the blessedness of the eternal depths with an undivided heart will look into the eyes of its source. 'Blessed are the peacemakers, for they shall be called sons of God'[16]: those who seek peace in their own hearts and the hearts of those around them will be the adopted brothers and sisters of the prince of peace. As children of God they will make his peace and goodness present in the world. 'Blessed are those who are persecuted for righteousness' sake, for theirs is the kingdom of heaven'[17]: those who suffer in the outer world for the sake of what is right will themselves reign in the inner world where God is king – God will be born in them.

The chart of the beatitudes shows us, by mapping the inner values that are to guide our outer actions, the treasure deep in the heart where God dwells. If the heart enters its own inner depths, looks into the ground of its being, it there finds the treasure, finds God, source of peace and of all good deeds. The kingdom of heaven is within us.[18] We need only to decide that this is what we shall value. 'Where your treasure is, there will your heart be also'[19]: to treasure God is to find him with the heart. He is won by love, a love that turns away from enslavement to the world to find the inner strength, the indwelling divine strength that can alone redeem the world. To win the absolute, an absolute renunciation of seeking life in the outward is needed, to find the treasure within. As St Augustine says, the kingdom of heaven costs whatever you have. The finding of God is 'A condition of complete simplicity (Costing not less than everything)'.[20] Every expectation of return from what is passing is to be exchanged for simply placing all our hope in God, like the man finding a treasure hidden in a field and, in his joy, going and selling all that he has and buying that field.[21]

Everything that has been said here about the beatitudes is summed up in the first beatitude: 'Blessed are the poor in spirit, for theirs is the kingdom of God'.[22] It is considered after the others because it summarises them, and the whole attitude that they teach, not because it is less important. Indeed, its importance is such that most of the next chapter will be exploring its implications. Here we will simply look at a fictional example of one who has the attitude that it teaches. In

Graham Greene's novel *The Power and the Glory*, the main character is a priest. He goes back to a country where priests are forbidden, to help a dying man. He is sentenced to be shot. These are his last thoughts before he dies:

> What an impossible fellow I am, he thought, and how useless. I have done nothing for anybody. I might just as well have never lived. His parents were dead – soon he wouldn't even be a memory – perhaps after all he was not at the moment afraid of damnation – even the fear of pain was in the background. He felt only an immense disappointment because he had to go to God empty-handed, with nothing done at all. It seemed to him, at that moment, that it would have been quite easy to be a saint. It would only have needed a little self-restraint and a little courage. He felt like someone who has missed happiness by seconds at an appointed place. He knew now that at the end there was only one thing that counted – to be a saint.[23]

This man has the exclusive priority of being a saint, of letting God come to birth within him. He does not look to anything in his outer life to justify himself: he looks only to God. He lays no claim to any good deeds. He has no illusions about himself being anything, so there are no barriers between him and God. That is what being poor in spirit means: having no illusions, claiming no righteousness for oneself. It means admitting the truth: the power and the glory come from God and not from the self. The priest dies a martyr for God.

In poverty of spirit the soul is prepared for the inner birth of God. The outer emptiness conceals the inner miracle. The dry bones hear the word of the Lord:

Behold I will cause breath to enter you, and you shall live. And I will lay sinews upon you, and will cause flesh to come upon you, and cover you with skin, and put breath in you, and you shall live; and you shall know that I am the Lord.[24]

God's power is known in his gift of unlimited life. The timbers of the wreck will be raised from the deep.

CHAPTER FIVE

NAKEDNESS OF SPIRIT

*Blessed are the poor in spirit, for theirs is
the kingdom of heaven.* Matthew 5:3

The first beatitude sums up all eight beatitudes, which
sum up the sermon on the mount, which is a summary of
the teaching of Jesus. It therefore merits close attention.
Each of the main words has implications in the original
Greek text that cannot be brought out in a single
translation. These implications have a spiritual
significance that makes them worth dwelling on.

The word for 'blessed' is also translated as 'happy'. This
lacks the important connotations of 'blessed', which
implies something holy, of rare, celestial dignity. The
Latin translation *beatus* is the same word from which
'beatification' comes. This tells us that the blessedness of
the beatitudes is that of saintliness. These connotations are
lacking from 'happy', at least as it is now currently used.
However this translation does have the merit of drawing
our attention to the fact that this is a state to be enjoyed in
this life, not only in heaven. While blessedness is
associated with heaven, happiness is to be known here
and now. The whole of the beatitude, including the
promise of the second part, is in the present tense. Using
the word 'happy' reminds us that it is the transformation
of our present life, as well as eternal blessedness in
heaven, that is being discussed. However, to avoid banal
associations, we need to distinguish what sort of
happiness is meant. Clearly it is not merely the sort of
happiness that someone enjoys because they are asleep or
because of a good bottle of wine. Neither is it the
'happiness' of having fun or being entertained. (Indeed,
we could say that these uses are a corruption of the word.)

It is rather the sort of happiness that is derived from doing something good, like helping people. It is true happiness (sometimes called fulfilment). It does not depend on any illusion. St Ignatius, in his rules for spiritual discernment, identifies this sort of happiness as a guide to action. If someone is fundamentally oriented towards God, when they feel a happiness like this in considering a particular course of action, they know they are on the right track. It is the opposite of the evil glee that those who have turned from God take in their ill deeds. It is the joy Jesus speaks of when he says, 'Your hearts will rejoice, and no one will take your joy from you'.[1]

This is promised to those who are 'poor in spirit'. The word that is translated as 'poor' can also be rendered as 'beggars'. This has the important implication that not only do such people have nothing of their own: they are also in need and have to ask for what they need, relying on the goodness of another. In fact, everyone is in need in the sense that their holiness and happiness cannot come from themselves but only from God. What distinguishes the saints is that they *know* this and turn expectantly to God with the trust that he will fulfil their need, and the humility to acknowledge it. The humility is made possible by the trust, just as we find we are able to be open about our weaknesses with somebody who we are confident will be supportive, rather than taking advantage of them.

The word rendered as 'in spirit' can also be rendered 'interiorly'. This helps us to see the range of meanings of what is normally translated as 'poor in spirit'. The implication of the latter translation is that the blessed are those who are not attached to material things. They may own or have the use of quite a lot, but there is nothing they are unwilling to give up if a greater good (such as the welfare of their neighbour) demands it. This is an important part of the meaning, but it is not the whole story of the holiness that is being taught. If instead we render the phrase as 'inwardly beggars', it can be seen as not just referring to a lack of attachment and possessiveness with regard to outward (material) goods but also as meaning an absence of claim to ownership of inward goods, such as virtues and spiritual gifts. How important a part of holiness this is becomes clear when we think about those who do lay claim to their virtues, the self-righteous. This category of person is that least gently spoken about by Jesus in the gospels, as, for example, when he tells a parable 'to those who trusted in themselves that they were righteous and despised others' in which the boastful pharisee is unfavourably compared with the humble tax collector.[2] Great delight is taken in their exposure on the stage, as with Shakespeare's depiction of Malvolio in *Twelfth Night* and Angelo in *Measure for Measure*. They are painfully difficult people to live with. The reason for this is that they mistake themselves for God. Goodness, they delude themselves, comes from themselves. Whatever their accomplishments, this claim to ownership of what is good in themselves all too readily translates itself into a tendency to claim the right to decide what is good for others, contrasting their good with others' bad.

On the other hand, saints, who are inwardly beggars, know that there is only one who is good, God alone.[3] They are full of gratitude not only for what God has given them in the way of virtue, but also for what God has given others. In both cases they receive this goodness as sheer and undeserved gift. Gratitude is a special mark of a good character. It acknowledges a person's true relation to God, as one who receives. In doing this, it removes the fundamental barrier: thinking one doesn't need him. This is why the medieval mystic, Eckhart, said, 'If a man had no more to do with God than to be thankful, that would suffice'.[4] The saint's gratitude encompasses spiritual, moral, intellectual and material goods. He or she recognises that nothing comes from his or her self. All is a gift from God, therefore all of it – from the meanest flower that blows[5] to the most prodigious manifestations of holiness – is a source of the greatest delight. To realise this is to be enlightened as to what is really going on and to reach the blessedness of the first beatitude, which is the delight taken in endless gifts from one who is wonderfully loving and much loved.

It is more than this, however. The second part of the beatitude identifies the blessedness of the poor in spirit as coming from the possession of the kingdom of heaven. Those who are willing to renounce all ownership (of material, moral and spiritual goods) will be given possession of the unlimited good of the kingdom of heaven. Hence Jesus enjoins, 'Sell your possessions, and give alms; provide yourselves with purses that do not grow old, with a treasure in the heavens that does not fail, where no thief approaches and no moth destroys'.[6] There is a small reflection of this process of renouncing ownership and being given the kingdom in the fact that it is much easier to give somebody something (or help them) if they don't take it for granted; that is, if they acknowledge it as a gift. As with small gifts, so it is with the greatest gift of the kingdom. The person who is willing to lose their life (that is, not claim it as their own) will find it (that is, be given it by God).

The word 'kingdom' may suggest that this life is given by an entry visa to an exceptionally pleasantly environed country, but there is more to it than this. The word that is translated by 'kingdom' can also be rendered as 'kingly power'. It is this word that is used in St John's gospel when Jesus says to Pilate, 'My kingship is not of this world'.[7] This suggests that it is the kingly power of Jesus himself that is being offered to the poor of spirit. This interpretation is given weight by the fact that the equivalent phrase in St Mark and St Luke's gospels to St Matthew's 'the kingdom of heaven' is 'the kingdom of God'.[8] What in fact is being offered to the poor in spirit, those who are inwardly beggars, is nothing less than the birth of God in the soul. This is a possibility of this life (it *is* theirs, the verb is in the present tense). The saints – those who, inwardly beggars, accept everything as a gift from God – are given God's kingly power. This is how they can perform miracles.[9]

The first beatitude is the pivot by which sanctity is achieved. It is the summary in a single sentence of the whole of Jesus' teaching. If we were to seek instead a single object that summarizes this whole, we would find it in a crucifix. The epitome of poverty of spirit is Christ crucified. It is from the cross that comes the kingly power, received by the saints, of 'Jesus of Nazareth, king of the Jews'.[10] Those who have received this power most fully have conformed themselves most fully to the example of Jesus on the cross, and become perfect beggars in spirit. We shall consider two examples of such inwardly poor souls.

In the last year of her life, when she was dying of tuberculosis, Saint Thérèse of Lisieux wrote a poem which expressed the way in which she followed, in the words of Guy Gaucher, 'her beloved Jesus in his passion'.[11] In it she likens herself to a rose shedding its petals. The theme is that a rose which has shed its petals is without any pretensions about its ability to be an adornment. 'A rose without petals is simply thrown where the wind takes it', she writes, 'the petals are walked on without regret'.[12] This is an image of her giving up any claim to making any impression, to owning anything, as she faces an agonizing death. There is no arranging for pretty effect, no seeking any effect or result for herself whatever. The poem had been requested by a Parisian Carmelite nun (a former prioress). She was very pleased with it, but she thought that a final couplet was lacking, explaining that at her death God would gather up these petals to remake of them a beautiful rose which would shine for all eternity. St Thérèse replied, 'Let the good mother herself compose this couplet as she understands it, for myself, I'm not at all inspired to compose it. My desire is to be stripped of petals for ever, to give joy to God. That's all.'[13] This is poverty of spirit. To put in the desired couplet would have been to act as someone who takes, rather than as a beggar in the spirit, who can only receive, gratefully. This grateful receiving extends to everything. On the day that she wrote this poem, she was asked 'Why are you so happy today?' She replied, 'Because, this morning, I had two "little" pains. Oh! very sore! . . . Nothing gives me "little" joys, like "little" pains . . .'[14] Happy are the poor in spirit.

The other example of poverty in spirit we shall consider is St Francis of Assisi. For him poverty of spirit – that nakedness before God which is the goal of all spiritual life – was acquired first of all by complete physical poverty. He was married to 'Lady Poverty'. According to his biographer, St Bonaventure, he said, '. . . poverty is the special way of salvation . . . This is the Gospel's treasure *hidden in a field;* to buy this we should sell everything, and in comparison to this we should spurn everything we cannot sell.' St Bonaventure explains the implications of the latter: 'No one can be said to have perfectly renounced the world if he still keeps the purse of his own opinion in the hidden recesses of his heart'.[15] True poverty entails being unopinionated as well as being bereft of material possessions. The renouncing of the world is not at all a refusal to care for it: it is a refusal to be dependent on its limited satisfactions so as to be open to the unlimited grace of God. St Francis wanted nothing to come between himself and God.

He expressed this in a striking way when his father brought him before the bishop:

> He wanted to have Francis renounce into his hands his family possessions and return everything he had. A true lover of poverty, Francis showed himself eager to comply; he went before the bishop without delaying or hesitating. He did not wait for any words nor did he speak any, but immediately took off his clothes and gave them back to his father . . . Moreover, drunk with remarkable fervour, he even took off his underwear, stripping himself completely naked before all. He said to his father, 'Until now I have called you father here on earth, but now I can say without reservation, *Our Father who art in heaven,* since I have placed all my treasure and all my hope in him.'[16]

This is a very clear enactment of the spiritual standing before God as a beggar which the first beatitude teaches. In exchanging 'treasures on earth, where moth and rust consume and where thieves break in and steal' for 'treasures in heaven',[17] St Francis is reinvesting his hope where it cannot be disappointed. As a complete beggar, he is completely free to receive God's gifts. St Bonaventure comments, 'Thus the servant of the Most High was left naked so that he might follow his naked crucified Lord, whom he loved.'[18] He was 'released now from the chains of all earthly desires' and 'in a carefree mood'[19] enjoyed the absolutely graced poverty in spirit that Jesus on the cross both exemplifies and enables. The fullness of his identification with 'his naked crucified Lord' results later in his life in his receiving the wounds of Christ in his own person. In him God is born once more.

These two examples – St Thérèse and St Francis – show us the perfection of spiritual poverty. However, it is not suggested that someone has to be dying of tuberculosis, like St Thérèse, or receive the stigmata, like St Francis, to be poor in spirit. What is necessary is to have no possessiveness. It isn't only the Franciscan tradition which teaches this. St Benedict in his rule for monks speaks of completely uprooting this vice, ordaining that 'monks may not have the free disposal even of their own bodies and wills'.[20] The spiritual perception behind this is that in reality everything we have is a gift from God. If we treat things as though they originated from ourselves, we both misperceive them and put a barrier of complacency between ourselves and God. Hence every spiritual discipline teaches an absence of possessiveness – a detachment – that leads to spiritual poverty.

One way of describing this detachment would be to say that it is an absence of pretension. It is pretentious to have material possessions for the sake of show, with a view to impressing others, in order to make oneself be somebody: only God can do that. It is even more pretentious to act in what appears to be a virtuous fashion for the sake of show, with a view to impressing others, in order to justify oneself. Only God can justify a person. A good person doesn't want praise: they want to be praiseworthy. There is a parable about the value of the absence of pretension in Shakespeare's *The Merchant of Venice*. The would-be suitor of the beautiful Portia has to choose from among three caskets, one of which contains her portrait. There are a gold, a silver and a lead casket. If a suitor makes the wrong choice he is bound by oath never to marry: it is a life choice that is being made. If he makes the right choice he marries Portia. The one who chooses the gold casket discovers that 'All that glisters is not gold'[21] and the chooser of the silver casket is told, 'Some there be that shadows kiss,/Such have but a shadow's bliss'.[22] The hero is not deceived by 'outward shows'[23] and chooses the lead casket and is told 'Turn where your lady is,/ And claim her with a loving kiss'.[24] He has chosen 'not by the view'.[25]

Every Christian needs to make a similar choice, since its object is 'one from whom men hide their faces',[26] the suffering servant, Christ crucified. To choose him is to prefer spiritual poverty to empty show, to prefer outcasts and prisoners, who need our help, to the rich and powerful who seem able to give us help. The resurrection is our guarantee that it is a wise choice. Like the timbers of the wreck on the seabed, it won't *look* like a good choice. The suffering servant is despised and not esteemed.[27] The one who chooses him moves from having an 'image problem' to not having a problem through caring about their image: like him, they 'do not receive glory from men'.[28] To care about one's image is to give priority to a superficial, outward show, to be as laughable as Malvolio in his yellow stockings and cross-garters.[29] We are what we are in the sight of God, and nothing else. To see everything with his eyes is to see everything in perspective: to see the plant in the seed, to see the portrait in the casket, to see resurrection in the crucifixion. It is to see that it is good.[30]

This perspective is able to transcend the limitation of all partial points of view. To do this is to reach the heart of the comic spirit: to be able to laugh at whatever doesn't deserve to be taken seriously, not with a mocking laughter but with a loving laughter that embraces weakness with tenderness and darkness with light. It is a participation in the play that is at the heart of creation. Poverty of spirit knows the sorrow of crucifixion, but – for the same reason: that it is willing to let go of what is passing in a generous spirit of sacrifice – it also knows the gaiety of liberating laughter. In God, whose kingly power is present in the poor of spirit, the apparent opposites of laughter and tears come together. This laughter knows the cost of leaving behind what it transcends, and this sorrow knows the value of what is beyond what it leaves behind. St Francis bore the marks of Christ's passion in his body and the gaiety of God's joy in his heart.[31] Through the gift of tears and the gift of laughter, the sun rises on the land of 'the glorious liberty of the children of God'.[32] All partiality is transcended and we are led into the freedom of the resurrection.

CHAPTER SIX

WILDEST OF FREEDOMS

For if we have been united with him in a death like this,
we shall certainly be united with him in a resurrection like his.
Romans 6:5

The freedom of the resurrection, life unbounded by terrestrial limitation, is the birthright of every Christian. It is granted in baptism. Unless it is traded for a mess of pottage – an addiction to a lesser good which cannot of itself give life – it is a good to be enjoyed now, in this life, as well as in the fulness of life beyond death. St Paul says, 'All of us who were baptized into Christ Jesus were baptized into his death'.[1] This being 'united with him in a death like his' is an identification with him that shares his poverty of spirit, lives the life of which St Thérèse and St Francis are such outstanding examples. The 'death' is the withdrawal of the heart, the vital centre of our life, from what is transitory to what is eternal. This is not to reject or despise the goods of this world: it is simply to see that they are not themselves the absolute, and to deal with them according to values that are eternal. This refocusing is described thus by St Paul:

> We were buried therefore with him by baptism into death, so that as Christ was raised from the dead by the glory of the Father, we too might walk in newness of life.[2]

With the death (the losing of a limited life) comes 'newness of life' (the finding of unlimited life). This is a refocusing of the heart on the goodness of God – 'the glory of the Father'. Instead of trying to find happiness in transitory and outward things – such as the impression we make on others, or the size of our bank balance – we find it, through faith, in the utterly reliable goodness of God. This is not to say that reputation and money are bad, only that our happiness should be entrusted not to them but to God. To make our happiness depend on the goodness of God is to find the source of the unlimited happiness – blessedness, indeed – for which we were made. St Paul describes it as being 'alive to God in Christ Jesus'.[3] Jesus offers us the possibility of being 'alive to God': of being aware of God's fathomless goodness and drawing from it a joyful life that knows no bounds.

Baptism is the realisation of this possibility. The ceremonies that marked it in the early centuries of the Church bring out the awesomeness of this realisation.[4] It took place in the darkness of Easter night and involved complete nakedness (symbol of identification with Christ on the cross), complete immersion in water (symbol of being 'united with him in a death like his') and reclothing in a white garment (symbol of 'newness of life'). As with St Francis standing before the bishop, the nakedness is an acting out of the commitment to poverty of spirit. The immersion marks so complete an ending of a former, limited life as to make what follows a new birth.[5] The white of the new clothing represents reaching the source of all living, just as white light is the source of all the colours of the spectrum. Baptism is the transition from living on the surface ('partly living')[6] to living from the source of life. This chapter will explore the latter.

We have already looked at a text that contrasts it with 'partly living': 'The thief comes only to steal and kill and destroy; I came that they may have life, and have it abundantly'.[7] Here the robber of the sheepfold is contrasted with the true pastor. The robber takes away life, the pastor brings life. The robber enslaves the soul to something that cannot really give life; the pastor enables 'the glorious liberty of the children of God'.[8] An image of the difference between the enslaved and the liberated soul is given by the contrast between the arid artificiality of a city at its least beautiful (when it is not an expression of human civility) and the noble wildness of nature. The former is the outcome of people's drivenness (their compulsions; for example, that of amassing money); the latter is simply the way God made it. The former is bound by imposed limitation; the latter is open to the infinity of God, wild in the positive and wholesome meaning of not having its life curbed.

The contemplation of nature in its wildness gives a sense of the source of this life, the same source that gives the human soul her freedom. Wordsworth recorded his awareness of the revivifying effect of this contemplation in a poem written in the Wye valley. He attributes to the 'beauteous forms' of the 'wild secluded scene'

> that blessed mood,
> In which the burthen of the mystery,
> In which the heavy and the weary weight
> Of all this unintelligible world,
> Is lightened – that serene and blessed mood,
> In which the affections gently lead us on –
> Until, the breath of this corporeal frame
> And even the motion of our human blood
> Almost suspended, we are laid asleep
> In body, and become a living soul;
> While with an eye made quiet by the power
> Of harmony, and the deep power of joy,
> We see into the life of things.[9]

'The life of things' – the immanent presence of God – is the same as the life of the soul, the source of joy and meaning. The 'beauteous forms' are not themselves God, but they are ordered by God and so awaken the soul to his presence, which is her life. This awakening to God's presence explains how Wordsworth can see the feelings produced by the landscape as influencing

> . . . that best portion of a good man's life,
> His little, nameless, unremembered, acts
> Of kindness and of love.[10]

The 'best portion' is the love that comes from God. This is fostered by the joy-creating influence of 'the power of harmony' – God's harmony.

This influence is much stronger when it comes from a human soul ordered by God's harmony. The natural scenery, if it hasn't been interfered with, cannot but display this harmony, but the human soul has been given freedom by God, and so her co-operation with this harmony is much more glorious. A saint, in whom the source of human life is made visible, has the same power to awaken to God's presence that natural wilderness has, but in a much higher degree. The saint radiates the unlimited life which is present, in a lower order of being, in the beauties of unspoilt nature. The difference between a saint who is a source of life for everybody and someone who will do for others no more than they need to in order to keep out of trouble by conforming to the conventions of society, is suggested by drawing a contrast between the scene that inspired Wordsworth and a French-style, rigidly organised garden, with its patches of gravel and portions of turf with strict instructions forbidding their being walked upon. The garden, like the person, is only conditionally available to others and conforms to a pattern rather than manifesting an innate beauty. The difference between a saint and someone in the grip of evil passions is perhaps suggested by a comparison between an American National Park and the meanest streets of New York. Freedom and beauty characterize one, danger and ugliness the other.

All this is not to imply that cultivation and building are bad: simply that essential life is wild and that sanctity is complete openness to this wildness. It is being nakedly exposed to the absolute freedom of God, the source of life, joy and meaning. It is putting up no barrier to truth, 'the wildest beauty in the world', which 'mocks the steady running of the hour', coming as it does from an eternal source.[11] Life and truth are closely connected, and both are wild. Only that which is not built on a lie survives. Truth, like life, affronts the prejudiced and closed mind. It is always challenging

> And every moment is a new and shocking
> Valuation of all we have been.[12]

New life challenges what passes for truth, the conventional or remembered pattern, to yield to authentic truth. The refreshing directness of children's conversation shows up the conventionalities of adult discourse. The vitality that flourishes in the presence of the truth is seen in the spontaneity of children. It is the absence of false restriction.

This is not to say that sanctity is simply a matter of doing what we feel like, or that children need no guidance from adults. The wildness of sanctity, the wildest of freedoms, is wild because it is rooted in the deepest and fullest sort of life: divine life. It is therefore beautifully ordered, in Wordsworth's words, 'by the power of harmony', God's power. It is a vivifying and inner order, the sort that makes a daffodil, not the outer and imposed sort of order that makes a tower block of flats. It partakes of the freedom that St Augustine envisages when he says, 'Love and do what you want'.[13] Loving contact with the creator allows his creative spirit to order one's life with the same beauty that flowers are ordered. The misunderstanding that mistakes this wild and beautiful freedom for licentious indulgence of disordered passion is not new.

St Paul addresses it in his first letter to the Corinthians. He writes:

> 'All things are lawful for me,' but not all things are helpful. 'All things are lawful for me,' but I will not be enslaved by anything.[14]

Christian life is not ordered like a painting made by filling in with designated colours spaces denoted by numbers, but this does not mean that there is no principle of order. The order is like that which guides and disciplines a great artist: it comes from beyond the person and at the same time from within. It transcends a passion for this or that particular thing. The freedom from standardized directives ceases to be freedom if it is given up to allow a single passion for something less than God to take over the soul: this is being driven, being enslaved. Nonetheless, in throwing out the bath water of being under the control of addiction to something limited, there is no need to throw out the baby of the glorious liberty of the children of God. St Paul is correcting a false view of liberty, not attacking true liberty which is a participation in the freedom of God himself.

This liberty is fully achieved when the whole person, including the physical senses, participates in God's freedom. St John of the Cross describes the moment of this achievement in the last two lines of his poem, *The Spiritual Canticle*:

> And the cavalry,
> At the sight of the waters, descended.

He explains:

> 'The waters' refer here to the spiritual goods and delights which the soul enjoys inwardly

with God in this state. 'The cavalry' signifies the bodily senses . . . In this state the cavalry descended at the sight of the spiritual waters, because in this state of spiritual marriage the sensory and lower part of the soul is so purified and spiritualized that it recollects the sensory faculties and natural strength so that they may thereby share in and enjoy in their own fashion the spiritual grandeurs which God is communicating in the inwardness of the spirit.[15]

To sum this up he quotes a verse from a psalm: 'My heart and my flesh sing for joy to the living God'.[16] The whole person, spiritual and sensory, joyfully delights in harmony with God and shares in his freedom. This is a higher sort of freedom than that of self-control (which is itself a higher sort of freedom than control by outer agency). Here there is no effort of constraint, simply a delighting of heart and flesh in God. The Spirit is monarch in the soul, delighting and not just controlling the senses.

This freedom comes from within, from 'the spiritual grandeurs which God is communicating in the inwardness of the spirit'. It is a realization of the scope of the inner life: God dwells within. Its joy and freedom depend only on God, not on outer things. It is therefore free from the sort of limitation described in the aphorism: 'A slave has but one master; an ambitious man has as many masters as there are people who may be useful in bettering his position'.[17] It serves only God, who gives himself, heart and source of all life and freedom. It is not at all like the freedom brought by power and wealth. It is the freedom of the kingly power spoken of by Jesus when he said to Pilate after he had been seized and bound, 'My kingship is not of this world'.[18] It is not a freedom which depends on being able to go wherever we wish. If it were, people would not vow themselves to an enclosed religious life in search of it. The restrictions of this life, such as the vow of obedience and the regular hours of worship, help the person opting for them to find this freedom where it can truly be found, inwardly rather than in moving about.

It is a freedom that can be found even in prison. There is a moving testimony to this possibility in Brian Keenan's account of his imprisonment as a hostage in Beirut. He describes an occasion when he is brought an unexpected bowl of fruit:

> The fruits, the colours, mesmerize me in a quiet rapture that spins through my head. I am entranced by colour. I lift an orange into the fat filthy palm of my hand and feel and smell and lick it. The colour orange, the colour, the colour, my God the colour orange. Before me is a feast of colour. I feel myself begin to dance, slowly, I am intoxicated by colour. I feel the colour in a quiet somnambulant rage. Such wonder, such absolute wonder in such an insignificant fruit.
>
> I cannot, I will not eat this fruit. I sit in quiet joy, so complete, beyond the meaning of joy. My soul finds its own completeness in that bowl of colour. The forms of each fruit. The shape and curl and bend all so rich, so perfect. I want to bow before it, loving that blazing, roaring, orange colour . . . Everything meeting in a moment of colour and of form, my rapture no longer an abstract euphoria. It is there in that tiny bowl, the world recreated in that broken bowl. I feel the smell of each fruit leaping into me and lifting me and carrying me away. I am drunk with something that I understand but cannot explain. I am filled with a sense of love.

> I am filled and satiated by it. What I have
> waited and longed for has without my knowing
> come to me, and taken all of me.[19]

Like Wordsworth seeing with 'an eye made quiet by the power of harmony', like Blake seeing eternity in a grain of sand, he sees 'everything . . . in a moment of colour and of form'. The source of life that is manifested in a particular form fills him 'with a sense of love'. In contemplating the form, he is in touch with the inner beauty – within creation and within himself – for which he has longed. The prison, at this moment, far from limiting his freedom, directs him to where he can truly find it, within.

There are other, more explicitly religious, accounts of spiritual freedom in prison. Charles Glass in *Tribes without Flags* tells how his prayer became more altruistic while he was imprisoned in Beirut; Irina Ratushinskaya writes in *Grey is the Colour of Hope* about a fellow prisoner of the KGB:

> On the last evening of the hunger strike we all sit around the table with cups of hot water. Pani Jadvyga reads us some poetry she has written. She wrote it in her native Lithuanian, but she has translated it for us into Russian: how the Lord comes to us unseen this evening. If we could see him, we would move up the bench so that he could sit down with us. But although we don't see him, he sees us. And not just us, but our hearts. The sentiments are naive, the Russian grammar a bit shaky. But Pani Jadvyga was not writing for literary critics, and we are warmed by the shining sincerity of her unpretentious words.[20]

In her imprisonment she is aware of the presence of Christ and communicates it to others. So too was St John of the Cross in his imprisonment in Toledo, a time of spiritual growth for him and a time when he composed some of his most inspiring poetry. It has been described by a Carmelite writer as 'not a disaster but a pasch: a poverty that allowed a new, a deeper communion' and as making him 'the poor man who could know Christ's unpaid-for desire to love him – a companionship that is new, original, outside any anticipation, personal'.[21]

Both the sublime poetry of St John of the Cross and the unpretentious words of the Lithuanian prisoner bear witness to the truth of what Jesus said in Nazareth, when he read from the book of the prophet Isaiah. After he had read the words, 'He has sent me to proclaim release to the captives' and all eyes were upon him, he announced, 'Today this scripture has been fulfilled in your hearing'.[22] Christ the saviour offers us the wildest of freedoms; a freedom that cannot be limited by a prison; a freedom grounded in eternal love, freeing us from the limitations of time and space. He saves us even from the limitations of the self, from the parody of true freedom that is the dark side of individuality: isolation, a sense of life carrying on without us, of fragmentariness and loneliness.

CHAPTER SEVEN

BEYOND SELF

Jesus is Lord. 1 Corinthians 12:3

It is often said about some interesting or worthwhile activity that 'it takes you out of yourself'. Happy absorption is contrasted with glum or agitated self-consciousness. It may seem that what has been said about finding God within contradicts this piece of common-sense wisdom. This is not the case. God is both immanent and transcendent; that is to say he is both within and beyond. If therefore we find God within our self, we are at the same time going beyond our self – and beyond glum or agitated self-consciousness. Even the hastiest reading of the description of it by St John of Cross, *The Living Flame of Love*, indicates that calling this finding 'happy absorption' is an understatement, to say the least. However, the important division is not between inner life and outward activity; it is between one way of inner life and outer activity, and another way of inner life and outer activity. Glum or agitated self-consciousness can also be expressed in outward activity. To work with a person doing this is to feel that the joint task has become an enormous burden, that nothing is too little trouble. It is working under the shadow of what Blake called 'the spectre', a person's false, oppressive self.[1] The opposite attitude also expresses itself both inwardly and outwardly. Inwardly, there is joy and peace, a sense of calm and happiness. These qualities are brought to any work that is done. To work with such a person is to feel everything slip into place: one had not realised the job could be done so easily.[2]

What happens in the latter case is that what normally passes for the self, the ego, is being transcended. The action, or the inner calm, comes not from the ego but from what has variously been called the 'transpersonal self', the 'unconquerable mind', the 'Jewel in the Lotus', the 'diamond consciousness'.[3] A Christian who is acting or reposing in inner calm like this will use the words of St Paul: 'It is no longer I who live, but Christ who lives in me'.[4] The action, the calm, comes from within but also from beyond, from the indwelling presence of Christ whose Godhead transcends all creation.

To reach the point where every act, every moment of repose is like this is, obviously, the result of enormous spiritual growth. It is the point of the birth of God in the soul, symbolised by the raising of the wreck. Anything that can help us understand what this growth is like is therefore of value. An image of this spiritual growth is given by the natural, psychological growth of a child. This can be seen as having three stages. The first is when he begins to become aware of his mother as a separate person, but is still unaware that there is any mother but his own. The second is the realisation that each other child has a mother, as he does. The third is leaving his mother for a life that is no longer dependent on her.

Spiritual growth follows a similar pattern of stages. It is not suggested that these stages are a universal measure of spiritual development – obviously individuals vary enormously – only that they give an idea of the direction in which growth takes place. The first stage is being aware of one's own 'I', but thinking that it is the only 'I'. This is more commonly associated with youth, but a person of any age can be in this stage in one way or another. For example: a child can think only of his needs and desires; a young man can proclaim his own brand of idealism as the procrustean bed to fit which all others are to be cut; a middle-aged mother can cling to her children seeing them essentially as means of fulfilling her ambitions; an old man may not understand the possibility of other needs than his own. As with any schematisation of growth, a person can be at this stage generally speaking and still show some characteristics of a higher stage: clearly only someone whose extreme youth excused it would be allowed by others to persist in a state of absolute blindness to others' viewpoints – we are talking here only of the general trend. It is also possible to be for practical purposes (that is, as far as one's actions are concerned) at this stage, while being able to imagine – and indeed wanting to reach – a higher stage. Imagination of better things, and the cultivation of the desire of them, is valuable for growth.

It is not to be supposed that to be at this stage is to be bereft of all virtue. It is quite compatible with kindliness, and even thoughtfulness. There is a delightful illustration of this in the character of Mr Woodhouse in Jane Austen's novel *Emma*. He is an old man who does not really understand the possibility of needs other than his own. Nonetheless he is kindly and thoughtful. When he has guests to dinner, he is very solicitous for their welfare. Since he cannot imagine needs other than what he supposes are his own – to be very careful about what he eats – he does what he can to stop guests eating any dish that is at all substantial, pressing on them instead a little gruel or, at the utmost, an egg lightly boiled. It is left to his daughter to attend to the guests' real needs. However, it is too hasty a judgement to write him off as a monster of egoism. He is, as the author tells us 'everywhere beloved for the friendliness of his heart and his amiable temper'.[5] The generously considerate, like Theseus, Duke of Athens, welcoming the rude mechanicals' play in Shakespeare's *A Midsummer Night's Dream*, look at the intention, not the result, and therefore appreciate his kindliness. It is still a virtue, and to be the object of it (as one receiving a present from a child too young to make anything useful) can still touch the heart.

All the same, it is not a very high level of spiritual development. The next stage, which corresponds to that of the child who realises that each child has their own mother, is to be aware of other 'I's as well as one's own. This is to recognise others, not just in theory but in practice, as people with their own separate and different awareness and their own separate and different desires and wishes. Each is understood as being in effect an entirely new world since each contains in their own consciousness an experience of the entire world. This stage is perhaps more easily understood by imagining oneself as the recipient of it. To be with a person who has reached this stage is to know that one is respected. No conclusions are jumped to as to what one might have experienced, or what one might want, or what one might think – still less as to what one might be. There is a feeling of space, which allows one to blossom, to unfold according to one's innate potential. Carl Rogers' practice and theory of psychotherapy is based on the insight of the healing value of being loved like this. To be able habitually to treat other people like this – without in any way misreading who they are by looking at one's own needs and desires instead of being open to the person who is present – is to have reached a high degree of spiritual growth. It is the ability to be humble before the mystery of another human being. In practice this ability is often (though not necessarily) learnt through marriage. Once one other person has been understood as genuinely alive in their own right (rather than as a second-rate duplicate of oneself, or as a means of self-gratification), then the imagination is open to the potential of seeing everyone like this.[6] To understand another person like this is to have transcended the self to at least a certain extent. A merely egoistic perspective is now seen to have been limited.

This is a high degree of spiritual development, but not the highest. It is not the pearl of great price, the birth of

God in the soul. This is the third stage, which corresponds to the child being grown up enough to leave his mother. It is a leaving of the self for the kingdom, a response to these words of Jesus:

> If any man would come after me, let him deny himself and take up his cross daily and follow me. For whoever would save his life will lose it; and whoever loses his life for my sake, he will save it.[7]

This is the prescription for ego transcendence. Following Jesus is being drawn, by love, to the point where 'It is no longer I who live, but Christ who lives in me'.[8] This enables an escape from the trap of self-limitation, of being limited by the self. The self-denial or taking up of the cross daily is, seen from the perspective of its goal, a joyful liberation from this self-limitation. It is leaving behind pettiness and narrowness to be sufficiently large of soul to have room for and rejoice in the presence of God himself. To cling to all the narrowness of the ego is to lose this joyful presence, which is true life. To give up the narrowness (which, because the soul is invested in it, seems as though it is one's life) is to find the true life which God's indwelling, his birth in the soul, gives.

This movement from false life to true life can seem at first as though it is a death – a complete loss of life – because the narrow life (defined by the merely egoistic) is so much what the person concerned has got used to thinking of as life that when it is left behind there seems to be only emptiness and blackness. It is rather as though someone who all their life has lived in a completely urban setting were to be transported during the night to the countryside. The absence of tarmac seems to forbid walking; the absence of cars seems to forbid going out, and the absence of sodium lighting seems to forbid seeing anything properly. However, the dawn comes, with its birdsong, dew and freshness and with them the possibility of learning to love the countryside. In a similar way, when the excitations of egoism are left behind, it can seem that there is to be no more life, only a wretched emptiness and darkness. However, as St John of the Cross said, 'The endurance of darkness leads to great life'.[9]

To one who is willing to live in the emptiness and darkness there comes, like the sunrise, the dawning realisation that whatever agitations of life (perhaps once perceived as thrills) are absent, here in the 'emptiness' is the limitless, the infinite source of life. It is as though in a darkened room that at first seems empty the eyes gradually become aware of a person. That person is Christ.

The soul leaves the self (in the narrow sense of the word) to find Christ her bridegroom. It is a sort of home-leaving, to which applies the admonition of the bridegroom: 'Whoever loves father or mother more than me is not worthy of me'. This is spoken in parallel with and with the same import as the words, 'He who finds his life will lose it, and he who loses his life for my sake will find it'.[10] This is a loss of partial life in order to find infinite life. In this finding, all partiality is to be transcended, as Jesus said to the great multitudes accompanying him: 'If anyone comes to me and does not hate his own father and mother and wife and children and brothers and sisters, yes, and even his own life, he cannot be my disciple'.[11] From the perspective of the dependency of his earlier years, a man's leaving his mother seems like hatred, and yet it is a growth. So from the perspective of spiritual immaturity, renouncing all partiality seems like hatred, and yet it is spiritual growth. It is not at all love of others that is renounced, it is the self-limitation of saying 'My own (whoever or whatever) is all that matters to me'. To walk clear of ownership is to walk into the realms of unbounded love. The walking clear is a requirement for learning this love from Jesus, who is unbounded love incarnate. He says, 'Whoever of you does not renounce all that he has cannot be my disciple'.[12]

Ownership creates a false self, a self defined by cosmetics (whether literally or figuratively), by the parade of possession. This life thwarts the true self, which is present in love, that is in Jesus. What is commonly perceived as the self (the 'I') is only a shadow of the true self (the real 'I'), who is God. Moses receives a divine commission to bring the people of Israel 'out of the hand of the Egyptians, and to bring them up out of that land to a good and broad land, a land flowing with milk and honey'.[13] This is traditionally interpreted as symbolising emancipation from sin and entry into Paradise. Sin is living from the false self, defining the ego and its temporary possessions (which in truth belong to God) as the absolute. So emancipation from sin is abandoning the false self and instead acting from the true self, which is God. When Moses asks, 'If I come to the people of Israel and say to them, "The God of your fathers has sent me to you," and they ask me, "What is his name?" What shall I say to them?', he is told, "I AM who I AM" and 'Say this to the people of Israel, "I AM has sent me to you." '[14]

This can be interpreted in theological language as meaning that God has absolute aseity: that is, only he derives his being completely from himself, the ground of all being. All other beings are contingent, dependent for their being and freedom on his being. Only he can say 'I AM' in capital letters, because only he has an absolute 'I'. Only in him is to be found the integrity, the wholeness of the whole of creation. Only he can speak as 'I' for everything that is. By contrast, when a human creature says, 'I am' the being can only be, so to speak, in lower case letters, because our being is contingent and dependent. The sense that each of us naturally has of being *of our own right* at the centre of everything, so that all things have importance only to the extent that they affect us, is an illusion, doomed to disappointment and, ultimately, death.

However – and this is the joyful news that the gospel proclaims – we have the possibility of exchanging this illusory, disappointing and doomed-to-die centre of our being for God, who is both the centre and source of all being and also contains all being. He is, as it were, both the central point and the circumference of everything that is, the creator and judge of all. By giving up the illusion that our relative and subordinate 'I' is at the centre, we can live from the real centre. This life is one of total harmony with all that is. As St Paul said, 'in everything God works for good with those who love him'.[15] If we freely and sincerely say 'Thy kingdom come, thy will be done on earth as it is in heaven', then God's absolute 'I' replaces our relative 'I'. It is no longer we who live, but he who said, 'Before Abraham was, I am' who lives in us.[16]

This state, where it is no longer we who live, but Christ who lives in us, is sanctity. Hence Catherine of Genoa could say, 'My *me* is God; nor do I know my selfhood except in God'.[17] Hence St Thérèse could describe herself as 'a living monstrance',[18] making Jesus visible to the world. The poem in which she does this ends with a prayer which sums up the whole dynamic of spiritual transformation:

> My Beloved, come to live in me
> Oh! come, your beauty has ravished me
> Deign to transform me into You.[19]

Desire for transcendent beauty takes hold of the soul so that it is not satisfied until 'Me' has been exchanged for

'You', or, to put it another way, 'I am' (the illusory absolute) has been exchanged for 'I AM' (the true absolute). In God, the grammar of persons is transcended: to the aspirant to sanctity he is 'You', to the saint he is 'I'. Furthermore, to the saint for whom he is 'I', everyone else is also 'I', loved as the self. She or he has gone beyond the 'self' as it is normally known, to live from the transcendent self in communion with everyone.

The idea of a transcendent self is implicit in the basic confession of faith, inspired by the Holy Spirit, 'Jesus is Lord'.[20] If Jesus is Lord, then nobody's ego has a right to be the measure of all things: each self is subordinate to the transcendent self, the true self known through faith. To the self that is not subordinate, he is a sign of contradiction. To those who are not obstinate, Jesus's lordship is a sign of unity. This unity is symbolised in the one cup and one bread in the eucharist. It is a unity which participates in the integrity, the oneness of God. It is the sign of a sharing in the glory of God, of his indwelling presence. It is the answer to the prayer of Jesus:

> . . . that they may all be one; even as thou, Father, art in me, and I in thee, that they also may be in us, so that the world may believe that thou hast sent me. The glory which thou hast given me I have given to them, that they may be one even as we are one, I in them and thou in me, that they may become perfectly one, so that the world may know that thou hast sent me and hast loved them even as thou hast loved me.[21]

Jesus is in all his saints so that they are one, sharing the same cup, the same bread, the same transcendent self.

This phenomenon, in which one transcendent self is recognised through the spirit by many, finds an echo in the effect great art can have on us. An uninspired piece of writing or painting fails to move because it does not speak to anyone of what they inarticulately know to be within. If it does speak to them at all; it merely echoes the ripples on the surface. Great art, however, articulates something that is recognised by many, down through the ages, because it speaks of something that is universal to humanity, something both deep within the core of each person and also in every person. It speaks something, however obscurely, of God, and as it does so there is a recognition and a coming home to the true self. Jesus is our true self, our Lord. In him there is no division, no separation.

CHAPTER EIGHT

COMMUNION WITH ALL

As you did it to one of the least of these my brethren,
you did it to me. Matthew 25:40

The transcendence of the ego has the effect of breaking down the barriers between the individual and others. Because the centre for the individual has become not the relative 'I' but the absolute 'I', Christ, they are no longer thought of as satellites orbiting the individual, but as worlds in their own right. The golden rule of treating others as you would yourself is spontaneously followed. No longer is it a matter of having to discipline the self, making an effort to consider others as having the same value as oneself. One's self *is* the self of others, just as much as it is one's own. This is the joyful result of renouncing all that one has, renouncing ownership. Losing everything (all ownership) one gains everything: everybody becomes as oneself, one self – Christ.

That Christ is the true self in everybody is implied in the parable of the last judgement given in Chapter 25 of St Matthew's gospel. Here, the judgement is shown as revealing the truth about what was going on among individuals during their earthly life and the consequences:

> The King will say to those at his right hand, 'Come, O blessed of my Father, inherit the kingdom prepared for you from the foundation of the world; for I was hungry and you gave me food, I was thirsty and you gave me drink, I was a stranger and you welcomed me, I was naked and you clothed me, I was sick and you visited me, I was in prison and you came to me.'

> Then the righteous will answer him, 'Lord,
> when did we see thee a stranger and welcome
> thee, or naked and clothe thee? And when did
> we see thee sick or in prison and visit thee?'
> And the king will answer them, 'Truly I say to
> you as you did it to one of the least of these my
> brethren, you did it to me.'[1]

Here Jesus tells those that showed kindness to others that
they were really doing it to him. He, the King, is present
in those to whom kindness is shown and so welcomes
those who have been kind into the kingdom. In giving
they have given to Jesus the true centre and source of life
and so they are given in return eternal life, in full
measure, running over. This giving is, at the deepest
level, giving to themselves as well as giving to others:
others' joy – their food, their drink, their welcome, their
clothes, their visit – is their joy. Others are their joy. Jesus,
joy of man's desiring, is their joy: they joyfully give food,
drink, welcome, clothing and visits to Jesus in others and
Jesus in return breaks out of the depths of their own
souls, where he had been waiting to come into their lives,
and suffuses their hearts and minds with the radiance of
his joy. He gives them the wedding garment of his own
spotless and sacred virtue which admits them into the
celestial banquet where they share the joy of all the
saints. The seed of this joy is already present for us here
and now if we do so much as give a cup of cold water to
somebody who needs it.

It is such exercise of Christian charity – a cup of cold
water or just a friendly look to someone who needs it –
that establishes communion with everybody. God loves
everybody and if we allow God to emerge from the depth
within us where he dwells, that creates for us a bond
through his love with everybody. The nearer we come to
sanctity – to the birth of God in our soul – the stronger

that bond is. The bridge between us and others is also the bridge between heaven and earth. Where love is, there is God[2]: if we love others, God is present, incarnate in our love – Jesus is alive in his body, the church, which is the coming together in love of all those who are not their own, but his own.

St Thérèse of Lisieux prayed to Jesus on the day of her religious profession for this charity, which she described as 'infinite love without limit other than you, the love which is no longer me, but you, my Jesus'.[3] These words express well the way in which this love comes from a transcendent source, Jesus, rather than the self. In another context, she describes the latter love as egoistic and unfruitful. By contrast, the love that comes from Jesus knows no limit. It goes beyond the boundaries of the egoistic self to find Jesus, who is infinite God. Once liberated from imprisonment in the egoistic self, there is no limit to the good it can do. Another prayer written by St Thérèse asks for one's whole life to be nothing but an act of love.[4] There is a striking example of the scope and power of this love coming from the transcendent self, from Jesus, in the work of Mother Teresa of Calcutta who is named after St Thérèse of Lisieux.

She explains how her work comes from this source:

> If the work is looked at just by our own eyes and only from our own way, naturally, we ourselves we can do nothing. But in Christ we can do all things. That's why this work has become possible, because we are convinced that it is he, he who is working with us and through us in the poor and for the poor.[5]

Her work (that is, the work of Jesus) has achieved a recognition and worldwide expanse of the sort that multinational companies can only dream about. Yet it works in a way opposite to these and other organisations of worldwide scope. Instead of the impersonal, standardised and many times reproduced product, it offers a uniquely personal attention. The key, as Mother Teresa explains, is Jesus:

> I believe in person to person; every person is Christ for me, and since there is only one Jesus, that person is only one person in the world for me at that moment.[6]

Every person is Christ for her. She sees through the egoistic self, which she calls a 'distressing disguise', to the true self of each person, Jesus, the anointed one. She acts too from her own true self, the same self, furthering the kingdom in which the purpose of God is 'to unite all things in him, things in heaven and things on earth'.[7] Her work is, as is the prayer of Christians, 'through Jesus Christ Our Lord'.

To love like this, with the love of Jesus, is to be what we are made to be, for, in William Blake's prophetic words, 'Man is love/As God is love'. To be transformed like this is to have exchanged the painful limitation of inadequate and false self-love for the heavenly joy of true love. Love is our true self, and in loving God and others we find that self, find Jesus. There is no opposition between loving ourselves and loving God and others. The only opposition is that between being loving and being unloving: that is the great divide. As the shepherd divides the sheep from the goats, so will the King divide the loving from the unloving, and to the blessed of the Father – those who live from their true self, love – he will say 'Inherit the kingdom prepared for you from the foundation of the world' and 'As you did it to one of the least of these my brethren, you did it to me,'[8] because to love another is to love Christ, is to love our true self truly.

Love is undivided: we cannot refuse to love God and others and still love ourselves. All this refusal achieves is to exile ourselves from our true selves, to exile ourselves from love itself so that we can only hear the voice of love as the blazing roar of 'the eternal fire prepared for the devil and his angels'.[9]

However, that is not how we hear the voice of love in this life. We hear him urging us with infinite tenderness and compassion to love ourselves truly while there is yet time, to give that we may receive, in full measure, pressed down and running over. We hear him asking us to show his tenderness and compassion to those who are unloving, those who exile themselves from infinite love and mercy, so that we may be children of our Father who is in heaven. We hear him speak of the abundant life he has come to bring us, the life of love. Love, through love, calls each of us, just as we are, to love. He assures us that we get more out of this life of love than we put into it: a hundredfold now in this time, and in the age to come eternal life.

Indeed, in seeking his kingdom and his righteousness, we find all other things as well.[10] In God, nothing is neglected. If God is born within us, then living within us is the true owner of everything that is, its very source and substance. So all things belong to us, as they belong to our true self, to Jesus. There is a beautiful expression of this in Traherne's *Centuries of Meditation*, where he describes how things appeared to him as a child, and identifies this as the way things are seen by one who has entered the kingdom of God by becoming, 'as it were, a little child again':

> The corn was orient and immortal wheat, which never should be reaped, nor was ever sown. I thought it had stood from everlasting to everlasting. The dust and stones of the street

were as precious as gold: the gates were at first
the end of the world. The green trees when I
saw them first through one of the gates
transported and ravished me, their sweetness
and unusual beauty made my heart to leap, and
almost mad with ecstasy, they were strange and
wonderful things . . .

This is the world seen from the viewpoint of the true self,
of God within. It follows that:

Eternity was manifest in the Light of Day, and
something infinite behind everything appeared:
which talked with my expectation and moved
my desire. The city seemed to stand in Eden, or
to be built in Heaven. The streets were mine, the
temple was mine, the people were mine, their
clothes and gold and silver were mine, as much
as their sparkling eyes, fair skins and ruddy
faces. The skies were mine, and so were the sun
and moon and stars, and all the World was
mine; and I the only spectator and enjoyer of it.
I knew no churlish proprieties, nor bounds, nor
divisions: but all proprieties and divisions were
mine: all treasures and the possessors of them.[11]

This joyful perception of everything from the point of
view of God, who is immanent within it, is seeing the
world as God sees it, good and beautiful, rather than as
distorted human vision pictures it, 'a Babel of
Confusions: Invented Riches, Pomps and Vanities,
brought in by Sin'.[12] It is made possible by poverty of
spirit, by the abandonment of all ownership. This leads,
by the principle of losing one's life to find it, to essential
ownership of everything, which replaces superficial and
unstable ownership of some things. This is ownership at

a deeper level than that of the petty parcelling out of proprietorship. It is not that which exploits and destroys things: it is a communion, not just with all people, but with all things. Every perception is an experience of the joy of reciprocated love. This is because, as St John of the Cross explains in *The Living Flame of Love*, 'the soul knows creatures through God and not God through creatures'. The former is a deeper knowledge because it is 'knowing the effects through their cause and not the cause through its effects'.[13] It knows things 'better in God's being than in themselves';[14] there, they 'disclose the beauties of their being, power, loveliness, and graces, and the root of their duration and life'.[15] It is a knowledge full of delight.

The nature of this communion and this delight become clearer if they are contrasted with their opposite; isolation and anguish. These are the effect of 'the living flame of love' being outside instead of within. This is hell: to live so much on the surface of one's being that what is properly interior and the source of life, love and joy becomes, contrary to its purpose, exterior. It is the human person turned inside out. It is the use of the gift of freedom, which is (to an extent) a participation in God's own freedom, in implacable opposition to the divine purpose that we should live. There is a poem by Robert Graves that expresses something of this:

> The suicide, far from content,
> Stared down at his own shattered skull:
> Was this what he meant?
>
> Had not his purpose been
> To liberate himself from duns and dolts
> By a change of scene?
>
> From somewhere came a roll of laughter:
> He had looked so on his wedding-day,
> And the day after.

There was nowhere at all to go,
And no diversion now but to peruse
What literature the winds might blow

Into the copse where his body lay:
A year-old sheet of sporting news,
A crumpled schoolboy essay.[16]

The point here is not the suicide as such, but the refusal of life. The person concerned is faced with the result of his own choice (first stanza) which involved the refusal to accept the company of others as they are (second stanza) and the pain of interpersonal intimacy (third stanza). The result is emptiness (fourth stanza) and limitation (fifth stanza). The life-refusing choice entails, not the absence of life, but life restricted to limitations that make it a torture. The 'year-old sheet of sporting news' and 'crumpled schoolboy essay' are a symbol of these limitations: the limited intellectual range of the reading matter represents the trapping of the immortal soul with its infinite yearning in the contingencies that it could not transcend because it would not accept.

For every damnation is a failure in transcendence. St Teresa of Avila's vision of hell is suggestive in this regard:

The entrance seemed to me like a very long, narrow passage, or a very low, dark, and constricted furnace. The ground appeared to be covered with a filthy wet mud, which smelt abominably and contained many wicked reptiles. At the end was a cavity scooped out of the wall, like a cupboard, and I found myself closely confined in it . . . . . . In that pestilential spot, deprived of all hope of comfort, it was impossible for me to sit or lie down; there was no room to do so. I had been put in what

seemed a hole in the wall, and the very walls,
which are hideous to behold, pressed in on me
and completely stifled me.[17]

This horrible confinement – this failure in transcendence
– is the result of a life thwarted and bounded, unawoken
to its boundless possibilities, unawoken to God who
alone can satisfy the human heart.

This confinement takes place when the soul, like that
in Graves' poem, or like the man who buried his talent in
the ground, withdraws from what God is offering her.
She does not trust enough to see 'the sacrament of the
present moment'[18] as what it truly is: a token of God's
infinite love. She cringes from the 'duns and dolts'
around, unaware that precisely these people are willed
by God as the means for her sanctification, and so she is
limited by her own refusal to go out of herself in love.
Such a stifling confinement of the infinitely yearning
heart can also occur by its being implacably fixed on
what is finite and bounded by space and time. This is in
effect the same thing exteriorized: a refusal to admit the
fullness of life by clinging to a kind of security blanket. It
locks up a heart made for the boundless plenitude of God
in what cannot give infinite satisfaction, so that it is
'cabined, cribbed, confined'.[19] Even the whole world is no
compensation for this locking up of the heart, since death
will throw away its key. This is to find one's life to lose it.

The contrast between this and the way of communion
and love is suggested by the difference between two
scenes. In one, people are walking about on a warm,
sunny day in a town square. They exchange greetings
and news; they are relaxed and happy, pleased to see
each other. The square, as well as having delightful
gardens, also offers cafés and at these the happy strollers
sit from time to time to drink each other's health. The
other scene is the same square, but there are no flowers,

no cafés: only a limited number of parking places. It is the same warm, sunny day and this distresses people as they are shut in their cars. It is very difficult for them to manoeuvre their cars as they get in the way of each other. The only communication is the angry sounding of horns and, from time to time, collisions and quarrels arising from the difficult search for a place to park. The car symbolises the false, hard, superficial self: those trapped within are not happy, nor do they make others happy. Because they are living outwardly rather than in their inner selves, there are clashes. Those that are happily walking about are they who have transcended this self (perhaps they have left their cars on the outskirts of the town). Their orientation is inward and transcendent, and so they meet without clashing. Of such is made the body of Christ.

For Christ to become incarnate, he needs to be loved. He can be loved inwardly, in contemplative prayer, and he can be loved outwardly, in those in need. This love gives their essential identity to the two aspects – contemplative and active – of the way towards his indwelling in the soul. This way is one of integrity: it seeks him in whom everything is to be found and finds wholeness in him. It is the way of love which, as Plato said, is the pursuit of the whole. Like the young St Thérèse, it chooses everything, gives all for all. The model for those following this way is the model of integrity, Mary immaculate.

CHAPTER NINE

THE PERSONAL ARCHETYPE

Let it be to me according to your word. Luke 1:38

Mary was completely open to God. In her the Son of God was physically conceived. She is therefore the personal archetype for all those who wish God to be born in their souls, at once a particular person and a universal model. We follow her when we ponder in our hearts[1] what the Word of God has made known to us, the teaching of Christ. This teaching tells us how to be conformed to him so that he may be born in our souls. There are certain actions that are friendly to him and therefore his birth. We are to feed the hungry, give drink to the thirsty, welcome the stranger, clothe the naked, visit the sick and come to those in prison.[2] His own life is an example of compassion. It is also an example, in the desolation of Gesthemane and the cross, of how to endure darkness so that great light may come. Through the endurance of the darkness of calvary comes the Easter light of the resurrection.

There is a description of this gazing at the light that is beyond the stars, beyond all creation, in the medieval mystical treatise, *The Cloud of Unknowing*. The praying soul is told to focus all her longing on one simple word, such as 'love' and 'with this word thou shalt beat on this cloud and this darkness above thee'.[3] The darkness is dark in terms of what is created, but a loving longing for what is beyond it can reach the uncreated light. The contemplative endurance of darkness in what is created is intimately linked with the active work of compassion. When we help those from whom there is no return to be had, the absence of worldly reward is a kind of darkness. Jesus said, 'When you give a feast invite the poor, the maimed, the lame, the blind, and you will be blessed, because they cannot repay you. You will be repaid at the resurrection of the just.'[4] Christian hospitality looks beyond the darkness of the impossibility of reciprocation to the light of the resurrection. Christian love looks beyond the darkness in the exterior shortcomings of those it loves to the light of Christ within them, coming from their true self. Faith knows that beyond the limits of the created is the uncreated. In looking beyond the limits of creation – to God – we find the light that can shine before men in our deeds,[5] the motivation to go on loving joyfully even those who are to us Christ 'in a distressing disguise'.[6]

In looking into the darkness with faith we are doing what Mary did. Like us, she lived by faith. She did not understand God's purposes. When the boy Jesus explained his absence in the temple in Jerusalem by the words, 'Did you not know that I must be in my Father's house?'[7] Mary and Joseph 'did not understand the saying which he spoke to them'.[8] When Simeon said, 'Mine eyes have seen thy salvation which thou hast prepared in the presence of all peoples, a light for revelation to the Gentiles, and for glory to thy people Israel' with the baby Jesus held in his arms, 'his father and his mother marvelled at what was said about him'.[9] She did not know what was going on: she simply trusted God. That trust needed to be very deep when 'there was darkness over the whole land until the ninth hour, while the sun's light failed'[10] and the fulfilment came about of Simeon's prophecy, 'a sword will pierce through your own soul'.[11]

It is trust and love that bring to birth the risen Christ in our souls. In the darkness, we have to trust. If we reach out trustingly with a longing love, God cannot reject that love, even if a mother could reject the child suckling at her breast.[12] We re-enact the trust and love that Mary showed, in recitation of the Angelus. In saying it, we look with our own trust and love for the incarnation to take place in our own lives. Her puzzled response ('how can this be?')[13] to the angel Gabriel's announcement may be our own reaction to the promise of Christ that 'the Spirit of truth . . . will guide you into all truth',[14] but if we trust, as Mary did, then we too will conceive of the Holy Spirit so that we will act from our true self: the way, the truth and the life.[15] Mary responded to the angel's message, 'Behold, I am the handmaid of the Lord; let it be to me according to your word'.[16] We can share her openness to her divinely appointed destiny by praying with the psalmist:

> Behold, as the eyes of servants look to the hand of their master, as the eyes of a maid to the hand of her mistress, so our eyes look to the Lord our God, till he have mercy on us.[17]

We can accept, as she did, a life in accord with the word of God by praying in the master's words, 'thy will be done, on earth as it is in heaven'. If these prayers, attentively seeking God's mercy and his will, are rooted deep in our hearts, then the Word made flesh will dwell there and be seen outwardly in the love among us. Our lives will reflect that of Mary, first among the saints, in bringing the light of Christ to the darkness of our times. St Thérèse of Lisieux, in reaction against some of the things that she had heard said in sermons, said of the Virgin Mary, 'I'm sure that her real life must have been very simple . . .'[18] Our lives, if they are attentively seeking mercy and the will of God, will share that simplicity, that absence of pretension. It is this poverty of spirit, this humility that especially opens us up to God's grace. Just as silence gives God the opportunity to speak within us, so simplicity presents, as it were, a canvas to God on which he can paint his own design. It accepts created darkness so that uncreated light can shine in it. It eschews false complications that cover up indigence; it does not want to be any more distinguished than it really is. The triumph of humility (to use the title of a play by St Thérèse)[19] is celebrated by Mary's great hymn of praise:

> He has scattered the proud in the imagination of their hearts, he has put down the mighty from their thrones, and exalted those of low degree; he has filled the hungry with good things, and the rich he has sent empty away.[20]

This is the guest at the wedding being asked to move up to a higher place, while the one who chose it for himself is shamefacedly demoted.[21] The true self (the one true self of all humanity), who is the host at the celestial banquet, rearranges the seating: the false selves are scattered in the imagination of their hearts.

This last phrase is appropriate for the distortions of the false self. Clinging to an imaginary reality inflates the false self, impeding the birth of the true self. The false self sets conditions which have to be fulfilled on pain of a refusal to accept life as it is, which contains God's gift of himself and his love, coming to us in the particular circumstances in which we find ourselves. For example, someone may refuse to contemplate the possibility of happiness unless they are able to marry a particular person – even when that is not a realistic possibility. Or, on a more trivial level, they may refuse to make the best of things in a cheerful way because the weather is unpleasant. Implicit in this and other such reactions to circumstances is the assumption 'If only I had what I want, then I would be a perfectly cheerful and loving person'. This is an illusion. In a more or less attenuated form such an illusion is very widespread. It is as widespread as the people who are not saints, those in whom God has not been born.

This is not a reason for accepting it complacently. Rather we can work at escaping the illusion – at hastening the birth of God in our own souls – by looking at those exemplary people who have escaped illusion, to see how they regard the circumstances of their life. On the surface of things these circumstances are often by no means what we would script for ourselves. The saints are not luckier than us. They have a different attitude to their circumstances. They 'know that in everything God works for good with those who love him'.[22] Because they have responded to God's love with their own love, their eyes are opened to see every circumstance of their life as what, in truth, it is: an expression of God's love for them. What it means to open one's eyes like this is suggested by imagining someone falling in love with someone who is already (unobtrusively) in love with them. Before they fall in love, the little signs of love from the other person (a look, a thoughtful attention, a trouble taken) are not noticed, or if they are noticed they are not interpreted for what they really are. An attention the other person has given is simply a minor convenience. After they have fallen in love, however, each little attention is full of meaning and joy in a way that is incomprehensible to one who does not love.

In a similar way, for the saint who loves God everything becomes a token of his love; everything is the best possible gift. A saint is confident that there is love behind everything. Hopkins' poem *The Handsome Heart* observes this attitude of trusting confidence directed towards himself in the response of a child whom he wishes to reward:

> 'But tell me, child, your choice; what shall I buy
> You?' – 'Father, what you buy me I like best.'[23]

The child trusts the father's goodness. The saint trusts the goodness of God. This trust extends to believing in his personal love in even the most distressing of circumstances. It is more common however to be called to believe in his love in less extreme circumstances, to see blessings where the faithless see nothing in particular. There is a poem by Thomas Hardy, *The Self-Unseeing*, which gives a sense of the pathos of missing what is being offered by a particular moment. It describes a return to a past scene:

> Here is the ancient floor,
> Footworn and hollowed and thin,
> Here was the former door
> Where the dead feet walked in.
>
> She sat here in her chair,
> Smiling into the fire;
> He who played stood there,
> Bowing it higher and higher.
>
> Childlike, I danced in a dream;
> Blessings emblazoned that day;
> Everything glowed with a gleam;
> Yet we were looking away![24]

Hardy is not writing about the absence of faith, yet his poignant evocation of a time when 'blessings emblazoned that day' and 'yet we were looking away' gives an image of life lived without faith. Faith is an awareness of the deepest reality: God's fathomless and personal love for us. To live life without it is to be looking away, missing its intended blessings. Everything glows with a gleam – the gleam of the glory of its creator. It only awaits our animadversion. However, in an important aspect, Hardy's poem does not represent the condition of one who has lacked faith. For Hardy, the earlier joys cannot be recaptured, but life is always transformable by faith and its concomitant joy. Only after death can such a possibility be lost. Every life can be transformed by receptivity to what God wishes to give us, a receptivity that echoes Mary's response to God's will.

This receptivity prepares the soul for the birth of God. It is a matter of not getting in the way of God, being little enough to give him room. The poet Keats was thinking of such littleness when he said that Shakespeare had negative capability. Unlike lesser writers who are fettered by their particular concerns, even their obsessions, Shakespeare is able to stand back and let his characters be, let being itself come to life in his plays. Spiritual littleness, poverty of spirit, is the ability to stand back and let the ground of being, God himself, come to life. Its characteristic qualities, Mary's qualities – humility, love and trust – have an exterior counterpart in stillness, silence and darkness. Stillness is the absence of agitation and fuss drawing attention to the false self. It can characterise action as well as repose: the action that is done without any superfluous parade, where the left hand does not know what the right hand is doing.[25] Silence is the willingness to listen, to be in communion with the great love of God, and to return that love with a gift of self so complete that words would only make it more partial than it really is. Darkness, when it is freely accepted, expresses the willingness to let oneself be led, or to be left without knowledge of the greater reality that would make sense of what one is enduring. It also expresses the willingness to receive no public recognition for what one does.

The propitiousness of silence and dark for the birth of God is voiced in the words of the book of Wisdom:

> While gentle silence enveloped all things, and night in its swift course was now half gone, thy all-powerful word leaped from heaven, from the royal throne.[26]

Gentle silence is the characteristic of Mary's humble love for God, a humble love that is present too in every soul ready for the birth of God. The puzzlement of Joseph and Mary about what is happening in this birth is a kind of night, as is the obscurity of Bethlehem and the stable. So, for the soul in whom God is being born, there is ignorance of the fullness of his designs and an absence of public applause. God comes quietly, as he came to Elijah:

> And behold, the Lord passed by, and a great and strong wind rent the mountains, and broke in pieces the rocks before the Lord, but the Lord was not in the wind; and after the wind an earthquake, but the Lord was not in the earthquake; and after the earthquake a fire, but the Lord was not in the fire; and after the fire a still small voice.[27]

God is in the 'still small voice', as he is in Mary's stillness and as he is in the stillness of the soul possessed in patience. He is born in a silent night.

Of course God is always present in the soul. In talking of his birth we are describing the moment when he so takes over a person's life that it is in effect God's life that is now being lived. It is a new life, a new creation in Christ. It is the culminating moment of a process of continuing conversion. This process begins at baptism, but baptism (as observation confirms) does not make people saints at once. The moment of birth comes as a result of a commitment that pursues the quest with everything that it has and a trust which pursues it despite everything it lacks. Although it is sometimes spoken of as being the result of growth (or in terms of related metaphors) it is not something that happens aside from a determined and continued self-giving to God. People do not just grow into saints despite themselves. It follows that we are not talking about a normal spiritual life in the sense of what usually happens. It is however normal in the sense that it is what is meant to happen. The reason for focusing on it is to be aware of what is possible, to be encouraged to pursue it. By looking at what we have not reached, we are given a motive to become what we are not: to strive and yearn for God's life to be born in us.

The moment of birth is not necessarily perceptible. It is in one sense an event in time. There is a change: after it has happened, a person lives so much through the grace of God that a falling away, although not in principle excluded, is practically very unlikely, and, since God is infinite, this new life can go on deepening. There is another sense, however, in which the birth is not an event in time. In this sense, it is something eternal. The life is one beyond the bounds of time. It cannot be destroyed by death. Seen from beyond time, the moment of birth is the eternal destiny of the individual. The gospel is the proclamation of that destiny, offering freedom from imprisonment in limitation. Mary's example of humble trust and loving acceptance of God's will is offered to us as sign of our destiny of receiving God's life.

In a poem which she said contained all that she would preach about her, St Thérèse described Mary's soul as a 'humble and sweet valley'.[28] That suggests a natural scene of great beauty; illuminated by the shining of the sun from heaven. Being humble is no more really than letting the sun shine on us; the sun of God's celestial and beautiful light. It may feel painful at first as our sorry pretensions are brought to light, but in the warmth of that sun, the tender mercy of God, we can begin to turn from the emptiness of self and, forgetting preoccupations with our own failings, open wide the eyes of desire in a loving gaze towards God. We can invite him, and his joy and peace, to be born in our souls while we are here on earth, so that his will is done on earth as it is in heaven, and others too know that joy and peace.

CHAPTER TEN

MOMENT OF BIRTH

And the word became flesh. John 1:14

The birth of Christ in the soul, the consummation devoutly to be wished, is total personal fulfilment. It is the perfect flowering of a love so profound that it incorporates the beloved. It is at once deeply personal, of cosmic importance, and of incalculable consequences socially. Eckhart writes of the joy of it:

> All that could ever be conceived of delight and joy, of happiness and pleasure, is no joy at all when set against the bliss which is in this birth.[1]

Every programme for personal fulfilment and happiness is nothing but an empty parody of this true realisation of what a person is meant to be. Of this alone can it be said, 'No one will take your joy from you'.[2] Whatever struggles precede it, this joy is like that of a woman who 'when she is delivered of the child, no longer remembers the anguish, for joy that a child is born into the world.'[3] It is the joy of a new life brought into the world, the eternal, immortal life of him through whom it was made.

This birth is therefore an event of more importance than anything in the cosmos, because it is the uncreated coming into the creature, the infinite blossoming in the finite. It has incalculable consequences socially because it is a coming into the world of a love without bounds. It is a love of perfect service, following the example that Jesus gave at the last supper when he washed his disciples feet. It is the perfect love of which it is said, 'He who abides in love abides in God, and God abides in him'.[4] It is an entirely pure love, not in the slightest dependent on any return from those to whom it is given, and therefore able to work in the most extreme absence of response, where any lesser love would be discouraged.

Yet the power of this love is equalled by the gentleness of its coming. Christ comes as he did in Bethlehem, like a still small voice. St Bernard describes the mystery of his coming:

> 'His footsteps are not known,' as it is written. Certainly it was not by my eyes that he entered, for he has no colour; nor was it by my ears, for he made not a sound. Neither was it my nostrils that discerned his presence, for his sweetness mingles with the mind, not with the air. The sense of taste did not detect him either, for he is nothing that one eats or drinks; and touch was likewise powerless to apprehend him, for he is utterly intangible. How then, did he come in? Or did he *not* come in, perhaps, because he never was outside? For he is not one of the things that exist exteriorly to us. And yet how can I say that he comes from within me, when I know that in me there is nothing that is good? I have ascended to the highest in myself, and lo! the Word was towering far above it. My curiosity has led me to explore my lowest depths as well, only to find that he went deeper yet. If I looked out from myself, I saw him stretching farther than the farthest I could see; and if I looked within, he was more inward still. So I recognized the truth of the apostle's words, 'In him we live and move and are.' But blessèd is he in whom he is, who lives for him and is moved by him.[5]

This is the gentle dawning of the uncreated light, utterly beyond what can be perceived with the senses. He completely transcends the soul in whom he is born and at the same time is immanent within it, there at a depth that extends far beyond reach. There result infinite vistas, within and beyond. For the person 'in whom he is, who lives for him and is moved by him', the person in whom he is born, this infinite space is carried within.

This has enormous consequences for how the person relates to the world. How a person knows, and therefore loves, others (things and people) depends on the sort of person they are. For example, a grumpy person will tend to see others as having something wrong with them. Yet even someone with a pacific temperament will have their vision limited by what they can grasp, on the basis of their own experience and ideas, as being valuable. The only way to be able to know and love truly everything and every person is to have the infinite perspective of God himself. Someone in whose soul Christ is born has this. It is not a matter of having an encyclopedic knowledge of everything; it is knowing the essence of everything, knowing him in whom we, and all others, live and move and have our being. This knowledge, this birth, is as available to the simplest as to the cleverest: it is a loving open-heartedness which is all-loving, all-welcoming. It takes an enormous joy in others, in all creation; the joy of God himself who made everything and saw that it was good.

The birth of the Word in the soul is an awakening there of the inner meaning of everything (the Word *is* the inner meaning of everything) and concomitantly of the inner delight, joy and glory of everything. This is described by St John of the Cross:

> This awakening is a movement of the Word in the substance of the soul, containing such grandeur, dominion and glory, and intimate sweetness that it seems to the soul that all the

balsams and fragrant spices and flowers of the
world are commingled, stirred and shaken so as
to yield their sweet odour, and that all the
kingdoms and dominions of the world and all
the powers and virtues of heaven are moved;
and not only this, but it also seems that all the
virtues and substances and perfections and
graces of every created thing glow and make
the same movement all at once.[6]

This is the kingly power, the sovereignty of God that
belongs to the poor in spirit. Its wonder, and the
tawdriness of what people settle for instead, give a
compelling urgency to the preaching of the gospel.
'Intimate sweetness' is offered instead of the hollow
pleasures of sexual predatoriness, and the glow of 'all the
virtues and substances and perfections and graces of
every created thing' are offered instead of the petty
empires of power and money.

This inner transformation creates a heart filled
with love and gratitude that is, essentially, happy
everywhere and brings happiness everywhere. It is the
wisdom of Solomon, for 'God gave Solomon wisdom and
understanding exceeding much, and largeness of heart,
even as the sand that is on the sea shore'.[7] The sand that
is on the sea shore is an image of the infinite possibility
for knowing and loving that the birth of the infinite God
in the heart gives. If each grain of sand is a world and all
that it contains, then the heart enlarged by the birth of
God in the soul can cherish them all and not be filled.
This birth, this enlarging of the heart is the object of the
spiritual quest. St Benedict explains in the prologue to his
rule that though 'the road that leads to salvation . . . is
bound to be narrow at the outset . . . as we progress in
this way of life and in faith, we shall run on the path of
God's commandments, our hearts overflowing with the
inexpressible delight of love'.[8] The discipline of the

journey has as its outcome an overflowing inner joy that delights in fulfilling the precept to love others as the self.

We have the testimony of those who have reached this outcome. Saint Thérèse of Lisieux was able to say in her final illness, 'It's incredible how my heart seems great to me'. That she saw this as a goal for everyone, not just those in religious life, is clear from a letter written a few years earlier to a married friend, explaining the universal source of this enlargement of heart. She observes that their childhood days are passed and that they are now in the serious part of life, and comments:

> The path that we are following is very different, however the end is the same . . . to *sanctify* ourselves in the way the good God has traced for us.

She talks to her of the love in her marriage in 'the language of faith':

> The Jesus of your first communion has remained the master of your heart, it is in Him that you love the beautiful soul who is now only one with yours, it's because of Him that your love is so tender and so strong.

The source of this love is the same as that of St Benedict's monks. St Thérèse reflects gratefully:

> Oh! how beautiful our religion is, instead of narrowing hearts (as the world thinks) it raises them up and makes them capable of *loving,* *loving* with an *almost infinite* love since it must continue after this mortal life, which is only given to us to acquire the homeland of heaven where we shall find again those cherished beings that we shall have loved on earth.[9]

This perspective alerts us to another aspect of the enlargement of the heart that comes with the birth of Christ in the soul. The love that comes from it knows that there is no final separation. Indeed, since its source is eternal, every act and thought of this love perdures in eternity. It is a therefore a free love with no need to hold on to its object for fear of losing it. It is not insecure, clinging or possessive. It loves as God does, from within eternity, and so it reaches all that it knows and loves in its most essential, unfading aspect.

This is so even of the love expressed in a single encounter. To be loved by a saint is to be loved to the very core of one's being, to be loved in one's immortal depth in a moment of eternity. This is possible because it is Christ, the true and eternal self who is doing the loving. A saint can love person after person like this with a full respect for each individual's uniqueness, 'for Christ plays in ten thousand places'.[10] Without Christ, the true self, who is both loving and being loved and therefore a source of communion and unity, the encounter with person after person would be an impersonal routine. This is because the love would not truly reach beyond those the person loving considered to be their own, whether because of allegiance, likeness, or pleasure in or through them. Furthermore this love would not truly reach the depths even of those it so honoured. This is not to say that all true love needs to be consciously identified as coming from Christ, rather that it comes from the depth where is to be found the true self which, whether or not known as such, is Christ.

The gift of this love, of Christ himself, is therefore greatly to be desired. Mother Teresa tells us how it is to be received:

> Prayer enlarges the heart until it is capable of containing God's gift of himself. Ask, and seek,

and your heart will grow big enough to receive
him and keep him as your own.[11]

This enlargement of heart, true wisdom, is the goal of the
spiritual quest, of the asking and the seeking that the
gospel assures us will not be disappointed. When St
Benedict writes in his rule that aspirant monks are to be
tested to see if they truly seek God, he is asking for
discernment of whether they have set themselves this
goal, since this is the only way that God can be found.
God is not to be found through investigation of the
nature of the creation, nor through any of the senses, nor
through logical analysis of philosophical precepts: he is
found only when he is born in the heart or soul, in the
innermost vital centre of the being.

All Christian teaching and practice is directed towards
this birth: every celebration of Christmas is an
anticipation of it, every holy communion is an earnest of
it. The whole of the Christian journey, from the first
inspiration of the Holy Spirit through the struggles in
prayer and self-discipline to focus the mind and the heart
on the one thing needful, to the anguish of the birthpangs,
all leads to this moment of birth. Subjectively the journey
may not always seem to be leading to greater joy, love and
peace, but that is because the struggles to focus the mind
and heart involve exchanging values once lived by for
ever truer values – the pain, if such there be, comes from a
lingering parting with the old values. To set aside what
gives pleasure for the sake of what brings happiness may
bring disappointment to expectations of pleasure until
better expectations have been learnt. It is as though one
has to get used to seeing by the clear light of day (God's
daylight, as the Russians call it) after being accustomed to
artificial light. At first its brightness makes it painfully
difficult to see, but once the ability to see in it is acquired
there is no wish of going back to the old murkiness.

The pangs of birth may perhaps be sharper than this learning to see in a new light. This is because it involves a very radical and intimate dispossession in the sense that it is not merely gratifications that are being left on one side for the sake of something better, it is a *life*. This is the life that is to be lost for the sake of Jesus,[12] the life of the limited, partial self. Before the unlimited, transcendent, Christic life can begin, this has to be let go. It may be that this will seem like letting go of what is most valuable. This is an illusion: it is not values that are being let go, it is private *possession* of them. When private ownership even of what is best has been relinquished, the soul is free to receive the birth of God, as St Joseph received his birth, even though he was not his own child. What to the old habits of heart is a complete emptiness and darkness (because nothing is owned) is, at this moment of complete relinquishment, filled with the light of the world: God is born in the soul and his joy and peace and love are there to radiate out to everyone the soul meets.[13]

This moment is of such surpassing value that it is truly worth everything: all time and all things. It is a star saying to every wayfarer journeying towards it: 'Never, never, never give up. Even if you can take only the smallest and slowest step forward, keep walking, keep faith, keep courage'. People who are seeking the ultimate in drugs, sex, fame, power or danger are not misguided as to what they seek, only with regard to where they are seeking it: the ultimate exists and we are made for it. It is here, in this eternal moment, in the birth of the uncreated in the soul. This is the moment that justifies all the labour, all the sacrifice, just as the raising of the timbers of the *Mary Rose* from the waters of the Solent vindicated the hopes of the researchers who believed they could find and recover the ship. As that ship was brought out of the sea into the air, so the divine is made manifest in a human life.

To talk of this moment as a birth is not to deny that a Christian can have experiences of the presence of Christ which are felt as though they were comings and goings. The 'moment of birth' is a way of talking about the inalienable indwelling of Christ that Mother Teresa is referring to in the quotation above when she says, 'Ask, and seek, and your heart will grow big enough to receive him and keep him as your own'. The one who possesses nothing for his or her superficial self is given, to keep, the true self through whom everything has its being. The difference between this keeping and the earlier experiences of presence can be conveyed by comparing a courtship, where there are visits and exchanges of gifts, with the consummation of a marriage.[14]

Because this consummation is the entry of the eternal into a human life it is appropriate to think of it as a moment, since a moment is the nearest approximation in temporal terms to eternity. Eternity is the end of the separation both of time and of space; it transcends them both. The person in whom the birth occurs will, from a certain temporal – and possibly not precisely identified – moment, begin living a life that is utterly wedded to the eternal and that life will go on through a succession of temporal moments, but in its eternal aspect it will be as one moment. That moment will bring the light of eternity to the comings and goings of men and women on earth, the life of God to the workings of the world.

It is a moment out of time. Eckhart comments on this 'Now of eternity':

> Here God is rich, and this is the kingdom of God. The soul in which God is to be born must drop away from time and time from her, she must soar aloft and stand gazing into this richness of God's: there there is breadth without breadth, expanseless expanse, and there the soul knows all things, and knows them perfectly.[15]

The birth of God in the soul leaves the dimensions of time and space behind. In doing this it achieves a communion with all that is, compared with which all knowledge of history and geography is only the shadow of a shadow, and all longevity of life and travel are the merest trinket. It is a participation in the eternal life of God himself. It cannot be taken away, since, as Eckhart explains, 'Once this birth has really occurred, no creatures can hinder you; instead, they will all direct you to God and this birth'.[16] This is because of what St John of the Cross calls 'the great delight of this awakening: to know the creatures through God and not God through the creatures; to know the effects through their cause and not the cause through their effects'.[17] Everything is known through God and therefore nothing can take God away. One is wedded to the perfect source of being, and any news that comes to one is brought by that source, whose presence is a delight so transcendent that, whatever the news, it is perfect fulfilment.

CHAPTER ELEVEN

DANCING BEYOND TIME

When we cry, 'Abba! Father!' it is the Spirit himself
bearing witness with our spirit that we are children of God.
Romans 8:15-16

When Christ is born in the soul we participate in the life
of the Trinity; the Son's life in the Trinity becomes our life
since it is no longer we who live but Christ who lives in
us. There is an indication of what this participation
means in the account of the baptism of Jesus given in St
Mark's gospel:

> In those days Jesus came from Nazareth of
> Galilee and was baptised by John in the Jordan.
> And when he came up out of the water,
> immediately he saw the heavens opened and
> the Spirit descending upon him like a dove; and
> a voice came from heaven, 'Thou art my
> beloved Son; with thee I am well pleased.'[1]

This passage immediately follows John the Baptist's
statement, 'I have baptized you with water; but he will
baptize you with the Holy Spirit'.[2] This juxtaposition
implies that Jesus's baptism tells us something, to do
with the Holy Spirit, about our own Christian baptism:
our initiation into our life as Christians, a life that reaches
its fulfilment when Christ is truly born in the soul.

Our baptism comes from Christ who baptises 'with the
Holy Spirit'. This is the distinguishing feature of the
baptism that Christ gives: John did not baptize like this.
According to the Acts of the Apostles, it is a distinction
that St Peter remembers coming from Our Lord Himself.
He says 'I remembered the word of the Lord, how he

said, "John baptized with water, but you shall be baptized with the Holy Spirit" '.[3] And later in the Acts of the Apostles when St Paul finds some disciples who have only been baptized into John's baptism, not having even heard of the Holy Spirit, he baptizes them again and they receive the Holy Spirit.[4]

The role of the Holy Spirit in our own baptism can be deduced from St Mark's account of Jesus's baptism. The heavens are torn apart, the Spirit descends on him, he is identified as the Son of God. St Paul reveals the meaning of this descent of the Holy Spirit in our own baptism when he says:

> You did not receive the spirit of slavery to fall back into fear, but you have received the spirit of sonship. When we cry, 'Abba! Father!' it is the Spirit himself bearing witness with our spirit that we are children of God, and if children, then heirs, heirs of God and fellow heirs with Christ, provided we suffer with him in order that we may also be glorified with him.[5]

In other words, Jesus's baptism shows us the inheritance, to which the Holy Spirit gives us title when we are baptized. We realise it in its fulness with the birth of God in the soul, when we can say with St Paul, 'It is no longer I who live, but Christ who lives in me'.[6] It is a life that fully lived, shares both our Lord's suffering and his glorification. It shares in fact what is shown to us in his baptism: the tearing open of the heavens, the descent of the Spirit and declaration of sonship by the Father.

Our adopted sonship is implied in the prayer that begins 'Our Father'. It is a relationship of provident care, since what father, if his son asks for a fish will give him a serpent; or if he asks for an egg, will give him a scorpion?[7] It is a relationship of being specially cherished. There is a wonderful expression of this, this being told 'My favour rests on you', in a dream that St Thérèse of Lisieux had. She dreamt that the foundress of the Carmelites in France, Mother Anne of Jesus, came to her with a look full of love. St Thérèse asked Mother Anne if God was happy with her. She received in reply a look 'incomparably more tender' than the first and the words, 'The good God doesn't ask anything else of you, He is happy, very happy'.[8] This is what Jesus won by his birth, death and resurrection, and shows to us in his baptism and communicates fully in his birth in our souls: the favour of God. It is offered to all. It was accepted by St Thérèse, whose dream was a foretaste of her glory in heaven. It was accepted by St Peter, who bore witness to Jesus's intention that we should be baptized with the Holy Spirit. It was accepted by St Paul, who knew what it is to receive the spirit of sonship. It is the bliss of the Holy Trinity, the life of the Son in a communion of love with the Father through the Holy Spirit. It is peace, joy and love.

This communion can be seen as a dance. In an ordinary dance the participants will sometimes be so caught up in it that they will go beyond the time at which they would normally get tired, benefiting from a second wind. This is a shadow of the dance beyond all time, where the capacity for enjoyment never ends. Here there are no limits of time or of place. The joyful celebration of love is unbounded. There is no need for the lament of Troilus in Shakespeare's *Troilus and Cressida*, 'that the will is infinite and the execution confin'd, that the desire is boundless and the act a slave to limit'.[9] It is celebrated infinitely in the transcendence of dimension. There is no question of its coming to an end. Of these dancers we do not say

Golden lads and girls all must,
As chimney-sweepers, come to dust.[10]

Nor do they suffer from the frustration of being limited in place. Sublunary social occasions have the in-built frustration that if one is paying attention to one person it is not possible also to give one's full attention to another. This dance knows no such frustrations. Living in and through the heart of everyone's true self, Jesus, one is in a full communion where no one is out of the gaze of one's love and one is out of the gaze of no one's love.

Together, in this joyful communion, there is ecstatic adoration of the supreme beauty. The dance of the kingdom is celebrated as though by 'a sea of glass mingled with fire'[11] to 'the song of Moses, the servant of God, and the song of the Lamb' with the exultant exclamation:

> Great and wonderful are thy deeds,
> O Lord God the Almighty!
> Just and true are thy ways,
> O king of the Ages![12]

There is perfect integration with the divine, for:

> Behold, the dwelling of God is with men. He will dwell with them, and they shall be his people, and God himself will be with them; he will wipe away every tear from their eyes, and death shall be no more, neither shall there be mourning nor crying nor pain any more, for the former things have passed away.[13]

This complete and perfect joy is reached once the bounds of earthly mortality have been broken, but the life of which they are the crown begins on earth.

This life is integration into the Trinity. It begins with God's love and our realization of our need for it. In the Winter Palace in St Petersburg there is a picture by

Rembrandt of the return of the prodigal son. In it the father places his hands on the back of his kneeling son in a gesture of conciliation, mercy and benediction. St Irenaeus said that the Son and the Spirit were the two hands by which God created the world. They are also the two hands by which, whatever we might have done, he reconciles us to himself in love. This is the meaning of the doctrine of the Trinity: that God reaches out to us in love. He has sent his Son into the world and his Spirit into our hearts. Through his Spirit we know the truth of God's revelation of himself in Jesus and grow through his teaching in heart and deed until he is born in us, so that with him we call God 'Abba! Father!' and become God's adopted children.[14] St John exclaims 'See what love the Father has given us, that we should be called the children of God; and so we are'.[15] This is the gift of the 'God of tenderness and compassion',[16] the 'God of love and peace'[17] who 'so loved the world that he gave his only Son, that whoever believes in him should not perish but have eternal life'.[18] Nothing whatever can separate us from that love.[19]

If we welcome that love with our own, expressing it by following Jesus's teaching as he wishes ('He who has my commandments and keeps them, he it is who loves me'[20]), then God's own life will blossom and be born in us. 'The Spirit of truth',[21] the Holy Spirit, will be in us, and teach us the truth of Jesus's words, 'If a man loves me, he will keep my word, and my Father will love him, and we will come to him and make our home with him'.[22] Sister Elizabeth of the Trinity, a Carmelite nun, dedicated her life to letting this happen. She wrote, 'It seems to me that I have found my heaven on earth, since heaven is God and God is in my soul. The day I understood that, everything became clear to me and I wish I could whisper this secret to those that I love . . .' She described her prayer as entering 'within' and losing herself 'in those who are there'. The words of a prayer she wrote show her doing this:

> O my God, Trinity that I adore, help me to forget myself completely to fix my home in you, still and at peace as though my soul were in eternity. May nothing be able to trouble my peace or draw me out of you, my Unchangeable One, but may each minute take me further into the depth of your mystery.
>
> Make my soul at peace, make of it your heaven, your beloved home and the place of your rest. May I never leave you alone there, but may I be entirely present there, completely awakened in my faith, all adoration, completely given over to your creative action.
>
> O my beloved Christ, crucified by love, I want to be a spouse for your heart; I want to cover you with glory, I want to love you to the point of death. But I feel my powerlessness, and I ask you to reclothe me with yourself, to identify my soul with all the movements of your soul, to submerge me, to invade me, to substitute yourself for me, so that my life is nothing but a shining forth of your life. Come into me as worshipper, healer and as saviour.
>
> O eternal Word, spoken by my God, I want to spend my life listening to you, I want to make myself completely docile to learn everything from you; then through all the nights, all the emptiness, all the helplessness I want to gaze at you always and remain under your great light; O my beloved star, entrance me so that I can never escape your radiance.
>
> O consuming fire, Spirit of love, come upon me so that an incarnation of the Word happens

in my soul; so that I am for him an additional humanity, in which he can renew his whole mystery; and you, O Father, lean towards your poor little creature, see in her only the beloved in whom you have invested all your mercy.

O my 'Three', my all, my blessedness, infinite solitude, Immensity where I lose myself, I give myself up to you as victim. Bury yourself in me so that I bury myself in you, while waiting to go to the contemplation of the abyss of your splendour.[23]

As this prayer suggests, God's immense love for us is to be enjoyed now as well as in the life to come. Our faith in his love for us makes this possible. The recent *Catechism of the Catholic Church* explains that this is our vocation by virtue of our baptism. It says:

By the grace of baptism 'in the name of the Father and of the Son and of the Holy Spirit', we are called to share the life of the Blessed Trinity, here below in the darkness of faith, and beyond death in eternal light.[24]

Here it is participated in, but seen 'through a glass, darkly',[25] beyond death it is resplendent in the light. We are called to this life which transcends death. It was on the feast of the Blessed Trinity that St Thérèse responded explicitly to this calling. She wrote about her desire to love God and make him loved and summarised it by saying, 'In a word, I want to be a saint', adding immediately, 'but I feel my powerlessness, and I ask you, O my God, to be yourself my holiness'.[26] This is God's supreme gift, of being himself our holiness, that in his love God offers us. There is no greater destiny than this: to be one of God's saints.

To be this is to be for God, in Sister Elizabeth of the Trinity's words, 'an additional humanity, in which He can renew His whole mystery'. The life of a saint is 'nothing but a shining forth' of God's life. The superficial life has been lost so that the true life and light of the world may shine forth. This life is an ever further plunging into the depth of God's mystery, his heavenly life, and on reaching its mortal term becomes the contemplation of the abyss of his splendour.

This welcoming of us into the life of God, even if we are morally speaking so destitute that we would gladly eat the food of pigs, is the joyful news of the gospel. It is a full sharing, not a feudal dependency, as Jesus announces to those who follow his teaching:

> You are my friends if you do what I command you. No longer do I call you servants, for the servant does not know what his master is doing; but I have called you friends, for all that I have heard from my Father I have made known to you.[27]

The command is to love and to forgive; the reward is the communication of 'all that I have heard from my Father' – the communication of perfect love, and of knowledge of the ultimate mystery. God shares our humanity in Christ and we share his divinity in Christ. The doctrine of the two natures of Christ, human and divine, is an animadversion to the possibility of receiving this ultimate gift of a share in the life of God. God expresses his strong tenderness for us in accepting the frail tenderness of our flesh so that we can know his glory and his joy.

In sharing Christ's life, we become coded for eternity. We reach a state beyond ecstasy (the leaving of the body through the impulse of love) since our body itself becomes the sacrament of perfect love, sharing the holiness of the Word made flesh. We become particular embodiments of universal love. Each of us has the integrity, wholeness of God, a wholeness that makes us participants in the ultimate purpose of all of creation. We join in this purpose not with the false authority of one who imposes their will on others, but with the true authority of agents of the perfect will where our peace and the peace of all is found. This divine life, shared by the saints, is both immanent and transcendent. That is to say it is both present within the particular moment and action and beyond them. For example, God's life is present in the moment and action of tenderly wiping the brow of one ravaged by fever, but it is not dependent on them. His life is spoken in the gentleness and concern, but it would be there all the same if there were nothing to be concerned about. It is in the world, but not of the world. It speaks in every loving action, but its depth is in the silence.

One who shares this life has the perfection of both purity and desire. Perfect purity is total freedom from enslavement to anything that cannot truly give fulness of life; perfect desire is absolute commitment to the true source of abundant life. One who shares this life has a love whose home is beyond the stars and whose heart is in the smallest attention to another; a love which is born beyond time, bred in the deepest seclusion and manifest in the midst of the world's suffering. In this life, this love, we find the apparent opposites of detachment and involvement, distance and intimacy meeting in a perfection that can only be understood in the light of eternity.

It is a life perfectly in the present, yet both recalling Edenic innocence and anticipating the glory of a new heaven and a new earth. It is a life which expresses in its actions what it means, the love of God; and yet the full depth of this meaning, the unbounded love which animates this life, is revealed only in the glory that is to come. We are given some obscure knowledge of this through symbols that both reveal and conceal what they speak of, such as the symbols of water, light and sovereignty in the final chapter of the Bible:

> Then he showed me the river of the water of life, bright as crystal, flowing from the throne of God and of the Lamb through the middle of the street of the city; also, on either side of the river, the tree of life with its twelve kinds of fruit, yielding its fruit each month; and the leaves of the tree were for the healing of the nations.[28]

The life is God's own life, yielding abundant fruit and healing all ills. Because the city where this life flourishes enthrones God, it is beyond the reach of evil and darkness:

> There shall no longer be anything accursed, but the throne of God and of the Lamb shall be in it, and his servants shall worship him; they shall see his face, and his name shall be on their foreheads. And night shall be no more; they need no light of lamp or sun, for the Lord God will be their light, and they shall reign for ever and ever.[29]

Each inhabitant shares the identity of God, 'his name', and is filled with his light. Each has the sovereignty, the kingdom of God, which is promised to those who are poor in spirit.

CHAPTER TWELVE

THE WATCHING FLOTILLA

I will give him a white stone with a new name
written on the stone. Revelation 2:17

'A white stone with a new name written on the stone' is promised in the book of Revelation 'to him who conquers'. This is a name 'which no one knows except him who receives it'.[1] This suggests a unique personal identity which no one else shares. At the same time each person is said to have the name of God on their foreheads and to see by his light.[2] Another way of putting this is to say that everybody shares the same transcendent self, the Word of God, while also having, in God, a uniquely personal identity. There is both union and diversity: union in the common celebration of the glory of God, and diversity in having each a special contribution to make to the manifestation of that glory. This special contribution is the unique and irreplaceable destiny of each person. If it is not made, no one else makes it.

However, since it is a manifestation of God's glory and God is within each of the blessed, it follows that it is a manifestation joyfully received as though it were their own by *all* the blessed. It is both personal and a joy to everyone. The scene described at the beginning of this book is a symbol of the entry into glory of a human soul. When the wreck of the *Mary Rose* was raised from the waters of the Solent there was a watching flotilla of boats gathered around. They are like the souls in glory welcoming another vessel onto the waters of eternity. These souls are a family welcoming a new-born child. To each the new arrival is an intimate joy, the joy of the manifestation of the glory of their true inner self. There is no barrier of 'mine' and 'yours' that causes interest to fade, as though those concerned were parents attending a children's singing competition, waiting with barely-concealed lack of interest for their own child's performance to begin. Every soul speaks what every other soul wants to speak and can only speak through the soul that is speaking it.

There are some reflections of this community of joy in terrestrial life. There is the generous joy taken by the large-hearted in others' achievements and successes. There is also the real common benefit that comes from one person's spiritual growth. The common nature of this benefit becomes clear if we contrast it with a material benefit. Imagine a family with limited resources. If they have only one bathroom and one person has locked themself into it, it cannot be used by another person. If at tea, there is only one piece of cake left and one person eats it, it will not be available for another person. These limitations can cause tension if material good things are the only value of importance to the members of the family. Suppose however that a particular member of the family has higher goals: he wants to become a kind and patient person. If he succeeds and becomes such a person, this will be a benefit to him. He will have the happiness of being aware that people tend to smile when they see him and the advantage of being more employable. He will be nearer heaven. Nonetheless the other members of the family will not be any worse off for his advantages. On the contrary, when they hear him say, with genuine patience and kindness, 'Please use the bathroom before me if you would like to,' or, 'Go on, have that last bit of cake!' they will have the quiet happiness of feeling that things are as they ought to be. Furthermore the kindness and patience will be a blessing not just to the members of the family, but to all those who have anything to do with the person concerned and they too will treat others better because of the way they have been treated.

On the spiritual level there is a community of interest. Spiritual progress brings benefits for others, not just in the greater amount of help that the person who has progressed will give others, but also in the greater realisation of the presence of God. This is in itself a good for everyone. There is too the encouragement to spiritual growth that others are given by example: this is a good of a very high order, since the well-being of others depends on such growth. This community of interest obtains with regard to everything in the celestial realm: each good for each person is a good for all those in heaven. One way of trying to imagine this is to think of a celebratory party where every drink anybody consumes has the effect of making not just that person but the whole company merrier. Anybody's good is a good for everybody. It follows that anybody in the company of the blessed is experiencing a good that is virtually unlimited, since the good of all the saints (their virtue, their peace, their joy) belong to them as much as to those in whom the good is. This is because all is known and enjoyed through God, source, centre and home of all.

This complete enjoyment of all that is good even extends to what is happening in earthly life. This is implied by Jesus's comment on the parable of the lost sheep, 'I tell you, there will be more joy in heaven over one sinner who repents than over ninety-nine righteous persons who need no repentance'.[3] Any spiritual progress of those still in the land of exile is a source of joy to those in heaven. It is as though they are parents taking delight in the growth of a child in the womb, and looking forward to its birth.

This intercommunion of joy is an outcome of spiritual life transcending limitations of space and time. Because God, who is infinite, is the centre and source of this life, experiencing one joy (or one person's joy) does not exclude other joys. All joys are found in God. There is an obscure reflection of this in the way recent technology struggles against the limits of space and time, although it can never touch the infinite. It can to some extent echo celestial communication, as when, for example, millions are able to be inspired by seeing someone like Mother Teresa on television. However, in the material realm, there are material limitations: the millions watching cannot be seen as they see, or be understood as they understand, as they might be in a person to person exchange of love. Only prayer has access to the divine realm where personal reciprocity of communication and communication with many are not mutually exclusive.

Yet this is forgotten when humankind's sole good is sought in material mastery, which becomes an empty echo of the true good, the infinite God. However quickly one can cover distance, manufacture things, or acquire information, life remains mortal and its term is still its term. Even mastery of the whole world is not worth the only life that will go beyond that term: divine life. The collective effort put into this never-to-be-absolute mastery of time and space in this age is as though the instinct for the infinite has been perverted from its true purpose, which is undying life in the supernatural realm. So much technology looks like a fragile and false imitation of celestial possibility. Being able to telephone someone from an airplane is not even a consolation prize compared with being able, as a saint in glory, to answer with one's own efficacious prayer the prayers of the distressed on earth.

Answering prayers like this, being able to do such good, is one aspect of the total community that is achieved in the life of glory. There are no limits to this: God is infinite. St Thérèse of Lisieux had the conviction during her earthly life that she would spend her life in heaven doing good on earth, a conviction validated by subsequent events which have been referred to as 'a storm of glory'.[4] Miracles of healing are a sign of the life which Jesus offers in abundance; miracles of conversion are a sign of a return to the source of that life. Miracles of replication, such as that of Elijah who was able to say to the poor widow, 'Thus says the Lord the God of Israel, "The jar of meal shall not be spent, and the cruse of oil shall not fail, until the day that the Lord sends rain upon the earth" ',[5] and miracles whereby someone is able to be present in more than one place at once, testify to how this life transcends material and spatial limitations.

This infinite life knows no bounds. Once it has been realised, others are led into it. Nobody goes to heaven alone. The joy of spiritual maternity or paternity is part of the life. Abraham's descendants, as many 'as the stars of heaven and as the sand which is on the seashore',[6] are a sign of the consequences of a life of faith. The watching flotilla of boats around the *Mary Rose* could also be seen as a symbol of the many followers that a saint has. This is at its clearest when a spiritual family, generation after generation, issues from a life of holiness. This happens when an individual is a founder of a religious order. Their personal search for God, and his consequent birth in the soul, establishes a pattern that can be codified in a rule that will serve others as a methodical approach to sanctity. St Benedict, for example, established a pattern of life which has been efficacious for countless souls seeking God in a stable community. St Dominic evolved a way of life that is rooted in prayer and flowers in preaching; St Ignatius pioneered a life of service to the world that is not of the world; St Teresa of Avila brought to birth a life lived in community and contemplation.

These founders of orders are doing on a large scale what everyone in whose soul God has been born does: they show that sanctity is a real human possibility, not a wild and unreasonable dream, and they draw people towards it by the attractiveness of God who is in their soul. Rather, God draws people to himself through them: they become mothers and fathers to others in whom God is born. Among them there is the widest diversity of temperaments and experience, yet they are all united in the one God; they all share the same fundamental identity, their true and transcendent self.

Nothing, but nothing, can matter as much as becoming one of those in whom God is born. This quest is worth all that we have: it is worth selling all that we have to buy the field in which the treasure is hidden; it is worth selling all the little pearls that we value to buy the pearl of great price.[7] The very fact of having set out on this quest gives every moment of our existence a most precious value; every moment can be a deepening of love, a greater remembrance of the truth and beauty that is in the depths of the soul and longing to be brought to birth. It is not necessary that we should be doing great things, since anything, however small can be done with great love. Indeed, the complete frustration of all activity can be embraced with the greatest love.[8] Any and every moment can be both an anticipation of eternity and an expression of a dynamic tension towards the greatest of goals – a goal whose fulfilment will increase, not decrease, the possibility of others fulfilling it.

Reaching the goal is a real possibility for anyone in any circumstances – the only qualification required is that of being alive. Nor does it matter how seemingly distant it is. The very first person to make his own the path cleared by Jesus was a condemned criminal suffering in the last moments of his life, which was being ended by a judicial execution.[9] Someone who has never thought of God can, by a single animadversion towards him, start on a quest that will lead to a fulfilment beyond the wildest dreams of ambition. This fulfilment is unbounded life: life with no limits, whether of space, time or mortality. This is a life that is a participation in the life of God, creator of heaven and earth. God is infinite, so such a life can do infinite good. It can bring its possessor infinite joy, a joy ever deepened in the boundless vistas of celestial peace as it is doubled ever again in its sharing with person after person. It can know no limit, no end, because God, in whom it is found, knows no limit, no end.

The way in which this life can start here on earth can be represented by the symbol of raising the wreck of the *Mary Rose* because of the various associations that it has: exploration of the deep, recovery of what is hidden within, forgotten treasure, and the joy of achieving something that is the focus of so many longings. It can therefore represent reaching the state of sanctity that seems to hover between miracle and impossibility yet is the willed purpose of the all-powerful, waiting only upon our trust and confidence. It can also signify the final fruit of that state: the resurrection of the body in glory. As the ship seemed in its sinking to be lost for ever, so death of the earthly body seems to be the end, but 'God created man for incorruption, and made him in the image of his own eternity'[10] and the emergence of the reassembled timbers from the murk and the silt into the brightness of the day can be seen as a sign of the celestial re-embodiment of life.

Of course a wreck is not at all an adequate symbol of a glorious body. Nothing on earth can be, for

> There are celestial bodies and there are terrestrial bodies; but the glory of the celestial is one, and the glory of the terrestrial is another. There is one glory of the sun, and another glory of the moon, and another glory of the stars; for star differs from star in glory.[11]

Since this is so, it may be appropriate to represent the glorious body in a symbol that says something about what leads to it rather than something about its unfathomable reality. For this, a wreck is not an inappropriate symbol. It speaks of the poverty of spirit that leads to the kingly power of God, of the lead (not the gold or the silver) casket that contains the picture of the beloved, of St Francis's marriage to poverty that rejuvenated the church, of St Thérèse being 'stripped of petals for ever' and unleashing a storm of glory.

It reminds us that it is not in outer appearances that spiritual glory is born and that we are closer to that glory when the pride of self-sufficiency is impossible. Hence St Paul was told, 'My grace is sufficient for you, for my power is made perfect in weakness,' and was able to say

> For the sake of Christ, then I am content with weaknesses, insults, hardships, persecutions and calamities; for when I am weak, then I am strong.[12]

It is not necessary to be strong, respected, comfortable or fortunate to enter into the life that never dies. The essential is trust in God, a trust that looks into the darkness (whether it is the darkness of weakness, abandonment or affliction) and goes on trusting. This trust, in its willingness to forgo the support given by any created thing, finds the life that transcends all creation, like someone willing to drop something of limited value from their hands in order to have them empty to receive a great gift. It may seem a foolish trust,

> For the word of the cross is folly to those who are perishing, but to us who are being saved it is the power of God . . . For since, in the wisdom of God the world did not know God through wisdom, it pleased God through the folly of what we preach to save those who believe . . . For the foolishness of God is wiser than men, and the weakness of God is stronger than men.[13]

It is a trust that has been shown to us by God in person, that we might show it to him. In accepting the utter nakedness of spirit of the cross, Jesus both trusts us – trusts that we will understand the depth of the love being shown us – and gives us an example of how to trust. There is not a greater darkness than that endured by him, yet

> Of this night scripture says:
> 'The night will be as clear as day:
> it will become my light, my joy.'
>
> The power of this holy night
> dispels all evil, washes guilt away,
> restores lost innocence, brings mourners joy;
> it casts out hatred, brings peace, and humbles
> earthly pride.
>
> Night truly blessed when heaven is wedded to
> earth and man is reconciled with God![14]

We are invited to share this trust. In our own lives, whatever darkness of weakness, frustration or sorrow is in them, we are called to hope, hope in

> Christ, that Morning Star, who came back from
> the dead, and shed his peaceful light on all
> mankind.[15]

This is a hope that can empower a quest that will cost us all we have, but which brings us to the moment that gives us infinitely more. As we walk in the way of nakedness of spirit we are walking towards this moment. If we are seeking it, God is yearning for it with an infinitely greater love. Eternally, he reaches out in mercy to guide us to the point where we are ready to receive what he longs to give: a new name, a new life. As he came to earth to show us the way to him, so he wants to come to us that he may live in us his unbounded life. All meaning, all hope, all desire call us to the silence, the trust and the stillness where the eternal miracle happens: the birth of God in the soul.

NOTES

NOTES

PREFACE
1. *The Good-morrow*, p.70 in *The Elegies and The Songs and Sonnets* edited by Helen Gardner (Oxford, 1965).

CHAPTER ONE: RAISING THE WRECK
1. Galatians 2:20
2. *Something Beautiful For God* (London, 1971) p.146.
3. *Confessions*, Book Ten, chapter 6.
4. *Ibid.*
5. *Hamlet*, Act 1, scene iii, lines 78-80. This and subsequent quotations from Shakespeare are from *The Riverside Shakespeare* (Boston, 1974).
6. Chapter 64.
7. Matthew 13:45-46.
8. *Sayings of Light and Love*, number 32, in *The Collected Works of St John of the Cross*, translated by Kieran Kavanaugh O.C.D. and Otilio Rodriguez O.C.D. (Washington, 1979) p.670.
9. Matthew 25:14-30.
10. Matthew 10:39.
11. Shakespeare sonnet 129, line 1; *Lullaby*, p.128 in *W. H. Auden, A Selection*, edited by Richard Hoggart (London, 1961).
12. Luke 1:38.
13. 2 Corinthians 4:18.
14. Matthew 16:18.
15. Isaiah 49:15.

CHAPTER TWO: SEEKING AND FINDING
1. T. S. Eliot, *Four Quartets*, p.222 in *Collected Poems, 1909-1962* (London, 1970).
2. People with learning difficulties can in the absence of articulate speech actually have a very articulate *faith*.
3. This is a theme explored in George Steiner's *Real Presences* (London, 1989).
4. Shakespeare, *The Merchant of Venice*, Act IV, scene 1, line 185.
5. Victor E. Frankl, *Man's Search for Meaning: An Introduction to Logotherapy*, 3rd Edition (New York, 1984).
6. *Collected Poems, 1909-1962* (London, 1970), p.63.
7. *Ibid.* p.74.
8. *Troilus and Cressida*, Act I, scene iii, lines 109-110.
9. Matthew 13:44.
10. Genesis 25:29-34.
11. Luke 9:25.

12. An example of this sort of thinking is Gödel's first incompleteness theorem; see pages 95-97 of John Allen Paulos, *Beyond Numeracy* (London, 1991).

13. London, 1989.

14. As in the quotation from a letter from Hilaire Belloc to Katharine Asquith, quoted as a foreword to Siegfried Sassoon's *The Path to Peace* (Worcester, 1960): 'The Faith, the Catholic Church, is discovered, is recognised, triumphantly enters reality like a landfall at sea which at first was thought a cloud. The nearer it is seen, the more it is real, the less imaginary: the more direct and external its voice, the more indubitable its representative character, its "persona", its voice. The metaphor is not that men fall in love with it: the metaphor is that they discover home. "This was what I sought. This was my need." It is the very mould of the mind, the matrix to which corresponds in every outline the outcast and unprotected contour of the soul. It is Verlaine's "Oh! Rome – oh! Mère!" And that not only to those who had it in childhood and have returned, but much more – and what a proof! – to those who come upon it from over the hills of life and day to themselves "Here is the town." '

15. As well as the musical, *Half a Sixpence*, there is the Greek word for creed which in its plural can mean the two pieces of a coin which two contracting parties broke between them, each preserving one part.

CHAPTER THREE: THE MASTER

1. 1 Corinthians 12:3.
2. Chapter 16:15-17.
3. Matthew 16:18.
4. John 14:6.
5. Luke 9:25.·
6. Hence the saying in the Talmud to the effect that he who saves a life saves the entire world, which, in the film *Schindler's List*, is engraved on a ring given to the hero in honour of the lives he has saved.
7. Revelation 2:17.
8. Philippians 2:9.
9. Ephesians 1:11.
10. Philippians 2:8-11.
11. This above all: to thine own self be true,
    And it must follow, as the night the day,
    Thou canst not then be false to any man.
    (Act I, scene iii, lines 78-80) The theme of the struggle to be true to oneself is central to the stories of Hamlet, Laertes and Ophelia and their commitment to their fathers.

12. St Thomas Aquinas, *Summa Theologiae*, 1a. 8,2: 'All of God is in everything and in each thing.'
13. 1 Corinthians 13
14. John 10:10.
15. Chapter 7:28-29.
16. Acts 9:2.
17. Chapter 12:1-2.
18. A breakdown of this sort is described in the story of the tower of Babel (Genesis 11:1-9). The full restoration of a unified society, where people are no longer separated by the egoism of insisting on their private way of understanding experience, is the work of the Holy Spirit, as described in Chapter Two of the Acts of the Apostles.
19. Matthew 12:33.

CHAPTER FOUR: A LIFE BEYOND

1. Luke 9:24.
2. Luke 6:20-22.
3. Luke 6:24-26.
4. Luke 9:24; John 10:10.
5. This paragraph is indebted to Piero Ferrucci, *What We May Be: The Vision and Techniques of Psychosynthesis* (London, 1990) pages 69-70.
6. Romans 8:35, 37-39.
7. The part that suffering can play in this process is explored in my book *Paradise on Earth* (Kevin Mayhew, 1993).
8. John 16:22.
9. John 11:25.
10. Prologue, p.165, *The Rule of St Benedict*, edited by Timothy Fry O.S.B. (Collegeville, 1981).
11. John 12:24; Matthew 13:31-32.
12. Matthew 5:5.
13. Matthew 5:6.
14. Matthew 5:7.
15. Matthew 5:8.
16. Matthew 5:9.
17. Matthew 5:10.
18. Luke 17:21.
19. Matthew 6:21.
20. T.S.Eliot, *Four Quartets*, pp.222-3, in *Collected Poems, 1909-1962* (London, 1970).
21. Matthew 13:44.
22. Matthew 5:3.
23. Page 210 (London, 1975).
24. Ezekial 37:5-6.

CHAPTER FIVE: NAKEDNESS OF SPIRIT

1. John 16:22.
2. Luke 18:9-14.
3. Matthew 19:17.
4. Sermon 27, page 209, in *Sermons & Treatises*, Volume 1, translated and edited by M. C. O'Walshe (Shaftesbury, 1989).
5. Wordsworth, *Intimations of Immortality from Recollections of Early Childhood*, line 204, page 555, in *The Norton Anthology of Poetry*, 3rd edition (New York, London, 1970).
6. Luke 12:33.
7. John 18:36.
8. For example, 'The kingdom of heaven is at hand' (Mark 1:15) and 'Blessed are the poor, for yours is the kingdom of God' (Luke 6:20).
9. Sister Briege McKenna O.S.C. gives a contemporary account in *Miracles Do Happen* (Dublin, 1987).
10. John 19:19.
11. *La Passion de Thérèse de Lisieux* (Paris, 1973), page 195.
12. Thérèse de Lisieux, *Oeuvres Complètes* (Paris, 1992), pages 744-5.
13. *Ibid*. page 1395.
14. *Ibid*. page 999.
15. Matthew 13:44; *The Classics of Western Spirituality*: Bonaventure, *The Soul's Journey into God, The Tree of Life, The Life of St Francis*, translated by Ewert Cousins (London, 1978) pages 240-1.
16. *Ibid*. pages 193-4.
17. Matthew 6:19-20.
18. *The Life of St Francis*, page 194.
19. *Ibid*.
20. Chapter 33 of *The Rule of St Benedict*, edited by Timothy Fry O.S.B. (Collegeville, 1981), page 231.
21. Act II, scene vii, line 65.
22. Act II, scene ix, lines 66-7.
23. Act III, scene ii, line 73.
24. Act III, scene ii, lines 137-8.
25. Act III, scene ii, line 131.
26. Isaiah 53:3.
27. Isaiah 53:3.
28. John 5:41.
29. Shakespeare, *Twelfth Night*.
30. Genesis 1:31.
31. Related to this is the tradition of Holy Fools, or fools for Christ's sake, which is drawn on in Dostoevsky's novel, *The Idiot*, with its main character, Prince Myshkin, who has the quality of innocent simplicity.
32. Romans 8:21.

CHAPTER SIX: WILDEST OF FREEDOMS
1. Romans 6:3.
2. Romans 6:4.
3. Romans 6:11.
4. Details are given in Edward Yarnold, S.J., *The Awe-Inspiring Rites of Initiation, Baptismal Homilies of the Fourth Century* (Slough, 1972).
5. John 3:5.
6. T.S.Eliot, *Murder in the Cathedral* (London, 1938), page 19.
7. John 10:10.
8. Romans 8:21.
9. *Lines composed a few miles above Tintern Abbey on revisiting the banks of the Wye during a tour*, lines 22, 6 & 37-49, pages 523-4, *The Norton Anthology of Poetry*, 3rd edition (New York, London, 1983).
10. *Ibid*. lines 33-35.
11. Wilfred Owen, *Strange Meeting*, page 1036 in *The Norton Anthology of Poetry* (New York, London, 1983)
12. T.S.Eliot, *Four Quartets*, page 199 in *Collected Poetry, 1909-1962* (London, 1970).
13. *In Epistolam Johannis ad Parthos* vii,8.
14. Chapter 6:12.
15. *The Collected Works of St John of the Cross*, translated by Kieran Kavanaugh O.C.D, and Otilio Rodriguez O.C.D. (Washington, 1979), pages 564-5.
16. Psalm 84:2.
17. La Bruyère, 'Of the Court', *Characters*, page 107 in *The Oxford Book of Aphorisms*, chosen by John Gross (Oxford, 1983).
18. John 18:12 & 36.
19. *An Evil Cradling* (London, 1993) pages 68-9.
20. Page 124, *Grey is the Colour of Hope* (London, 1988).
21. Iain Matthew O.C.D., pages 141-2 in *A Fresh Approach to St John of the Cross* (Slough, 1993).
22. Luke 4:16-21.

CHAPTER SEVEN: BEYOND SELF
1. See *The Poems of William Blake*, edited by W.H.Stevenson and David V.Erdman (London, 1977), p.635: 'It is an empty imitation of a man, not his real self – and so tragedy follows when a person depends on the shadow instead of the reality'.
2. These two attitudes are explored more fully in Chapter Three of my book *Paradise on Earth* (Kevin Mayhew, 1993).
3. See Piero Ferrucci, *What We May Be: The Vision and Techniques of Psychosynthesis* (London, 1990), page 70.
4. Galatians 2:20.
5. Chapter 1.

6. Although any degree of spiritual development is attainable in any state of life, one might contrast religious life with marriage. A reasonably good marriage more or less ensures reaching this second stage, but religious life is undertaken at the risk of remaining at the first stage. The compensation for this risk is that the life makes it easier to reach the third stage. It is as though entering religious life is playing 'double or quits'.
7. Luke 9:23-25.
8. Galatians 2:20.
9. *The Collected Works of St John of the Cross*, translated by Kieran Kavanaugh O.C.D. and Otilio Rodriguez O.C.D. (Washington, 1979), page 685.
10. Matthew 10:37, 39.
11. Luke 14:26.
12. Luke 14:33.
13. Exodus 3:8.
14. Exodus 3:13-14.
15. Romans 8:28.
16. John 8:58.
17. Quoted in Evelyn Underhill, *Mysticism*, 2nd edition (London, 1911), page 474.
18. *Oeuvres Complètes* (Paris, 1992), page 702.
19. *Ibid.*, page 703.
20. 1 Corinthians 12:3.
21. John 17:21-23.

CHAPTER EIGHT: COMMUNION WITH ALL.

1. Chapter 25:34-40.
2. 1 John 4:16.
3. *Oeuvres Complètes* (Paris, 1992), page 957.
4. *Ibid.*, page 961.
5. Malcolm Muggeridge, *Something Beautiful for God* (London, 1971), page 107.
6. *Ibid.*, page 118.
7. Ephesians 1:10.
8. Matthew 25:34,40.
9. Matthew 25:41.
10. Matthew 6:33.
11. The third meditation of the third century, page 110 of Thomas Traherne, *Centuries* (London, 1969).
12. The seventh meditation of the third century, page 5, *ibid.*
13. *Collected Works of St John of the Cross*, translated by Kieran Kavanaugh O.C.D. and Otilio Rodriguez O.C.D. (Washington, 1979), page 645.
14. *Ibid.*

15. *Ibid.*, page 644.
16. *The Suicide in the Copse* in *Poems* (London, 1975), pages 127-8.
17. *The Life of St Teresa*, translated by J.M.Cohen (London , 1958), chapter 32, pages 233 and 234.
18. God communicates himself in the present moment in ways that can be compared with his self-giving in sacraments. De Caussade is an example of a spiritual writer who emphasises the importance of being receptive to what God wants to give in the present moment.
19. Shakespeare, *Macbeth*, act III, scene iv, line 23.

CHAPTER NINE: THE PERSONAL ARCHETYPE
1. Luke 2:19.
2. Matthew 25:31-40.
3. *The Cloud of Unknowing*, edited from the manuscripts by Phyllis Hodgson (Exeter, 1982), chapter 7, page 15.
4. Luke 14:13-14.
5. Matthew 5:16.
6. Mother Teresa, *Loving Jesus*, edited by José Luis Gonzalez Balado and translated by Susanna Labastida (London, 1991), page 73.
7. Luke 2:49.
8. Luke 2:50.
9. Luke 2:30-33.
10. Luke 23:44-45.
11. Luke 2:35.
12. Isaiah 49:15.
13. Luke 1:34.
14. John 16:13.
15. John 14:6.
16. Luke 1:38.
17. Psalm 123:2.
18. *Oeuvres Complètes* (Paris, 1992), page 1103.
19. *Oeuvres Complètes* (Paris, 1992), page 915.
20. Luke 1:51-3.
21. Luke 14:7-11.
22. Romans 8:28.
23. *The Poems of Gerard Manley Hopkins*, 4th Edition, Edited by W.H.Gardner and N.H.MacKenzie (Oxford, 1970), page 81.
24. Pages 23-24 in *Selected Poems of Thomas Hardy*, chosen and introduced by John Wain (London, 1966).
25. Matthew 6:3.
26. Chapter 18:14-15.
27. 1 Kings 19:11-12.
28. *Oeuvres Complètes* (Paris, 1992), page 750.

CHAPTER TEN: MOMENT OF BIRTH

1. Sermon 29, page 220 in *Sermons & Treatises*, Volume 1, translated and edited by M. C. O'Walshe (Shaftesbury, 1987).
2. John 16:22.
3. John 16:21.
4. 1 John 4:16.
5. *On the Song of Songs, Sermones in Cantica Canticorum*, translated and edited by a Religious of C.S.M.V. (London, 1952), pages 229-230.
6. *The Collected Works of St John of the Cross*, translated by Kieran Kavanaugh O.C.D. and Otilio Rodriguez O.C.D. (Washington, 1979), page 644.
7. 1 Kings 4:29, Authorised Version.
8. *The Rule of St Benedict*, edited by Timothy Fry O.S.B. (Collegeville, 1981), page 165.
9. *Oeuvres Complètes* (Paris, 1992), page 501.
10. *The Poems of Gerard Manley Hopkins*, 4th edition, edited by W. H. Gardner and N. H. MacKenzie (Oxford, 1970), page 90.
11. Malcolm Muggeridge, *Something Beautiful for God* (London, 1971), page 66.
12. Matthew 10:39.
13. The way of dispossession is mapped by St John of the Cross in *The Ascent of Mount Carmel* and *The Dark Night*.
14. This way of describing spiritual development is used in traditional commentaries on The Song of Solomon. It is also used by St John of the Cross in *The Spiritual Canticle*.
15. Sermon 29, pages 216-217 in *Sermons & Treatises*, Volume 1, translated and edited by M. C. O'Walshe (Shaftesbury, 1987).
16. Sermon 4, page 45, *ibid.*
17. *The Living Flame of Love*, commentary on stanza 4, paragraph 5, page 189 in *The Complete Works of St John of the Cross*, translated by E. Allison Peers (London, 1978).

CHAPTER ELEVEN: DANCING BEYOND TIME

1. 1:9-11.
2. 1:8.
3. 11:16.
4. 19:1-7.
5. Romans 8:15-17.
6. Galatians 2:20.
7. Luke 11:11-12.
8. *Oeuvres Complètes* (Paris, 1992), page 223.
9. Act III, scene ii, lines 81-3.
10. Shakespeare, *Cymbeline*, act IV, scene ii, lines 262-3.
11. Revelation 15:2.

12. Revelation 15:3-4.
13. Revelation 21:3-4.
14. Romans 8:15.
15. 1 John 3:1.
16. Exodus 34:6, New Jerusalem Bible.
17. 2 Corinthians 13:11.
18. John 3:16.
19. Romans 8: 35.
20. John 14:21.
21. John 16:13.
22. John 14:23.
23. Soeur Elisabeth de La Trinité, Religieuse Carmélite 1880-1906, *Souvenirs* (Dijon, 1921), pages 321-2.
24. *Catéchisme de l'Eglise Catholique* (Paris, 1992), page 65.
25. 1 Corinthians 13:12, Authorized Version.
26. *Oeuvres Complètes* (Paris, 1992), page 962.
27. John 15:14-15.
28. Revelation 22:1-2.
29. Revelation 22:3-5.

CHAPTER TWELVE: THE WATCHING FLOTILLA

1. Revelation 2:17.
2. Revelation 22:4-5
3. Luke 15:7.
4. By Pope Pius XI.
5. 1 Kings 17:14.
6. Genesis 22:17.
7. Matthew 13:44-46.
8. This theme is explored at greater length in my book *Paradise on Earth* (Kevin Mayhew, 1993).
9. Luke 23:39-43.
10. Wisdom 2:23.
11. 1 Corinthians 15:40-41.
12. 2 Corinthians 12:9-10.
13. 1 Corinthians 1:18,21,25.
14. From the *Exultet* in the Catholic liturgy for Easter Saturday night.
15. *Ibid.*

ACKNOWLEDGEMENTS

ACKNOWLEDGEMENTS

The publishers wish to express their gratitude to the following for permission to use copyright material:

Element Books Ltd, The Old School House, The Courtyard, Bell Street, Shaftesbury, Dorset SP7 8BP for extracts from *Meister Eckhart*, from *Sermons & Treatises, Volume 1*, translated and edited by M.C.O'Walshe (Shaftesbury, 1987).

Faber & Faber Ltd, 3 Queen Square, London WC1N 3AU for extracts from 'Little Gidding', 'East Coker' and 'The Waste Land', taken from *Collected Poems 1909-1962* by T.S.Eliot.

Oxford University Press, Walton Street, Oxford OX2 6DP for the extract from *Centuries of Meditation* by Thomas Traherne, edited by H. M. Margoliouth (1958).

HarperCollins Publishers, 77-85 Fulham Palace Road, Hammersmith, London W6 8JB for extracts from *Something Beautiful for God* by Malcolm Muggeridge.

Hodder & Stoughton Publishers, 338 Euston Road, London NW1 3BH for the extract from *Grey is the Colour of Hope* by Irina Ratushinskaya (London, 1988).

ICS Publications, 2131 Lincoln Road, N.E. Washington, DC 20002, USA, for extracts from *The Collected Works of St John of the Cross*, translated by Kieran Kavanaugh and Otilio Rodriguez © 1979, 1991, by Washington Province of Discalced Carmelites.

Paulist Press, 997 Macarthur Boulevard, Mahwah, NJ 07430, USA, for the following extracts from *Bonaventure*: 'The Soul's Journey into God'; 'The Tree of Life'; 'The Life of St Francis', translation and introduction by Ewert Cousins. © 1978 by The Missionary Society of St Paul the Apostle in the State of New York. From *The Classics of Western Spirituality* series.

Penguin Books Ltd, 27 Wrights Lane, London W8 5TZ for extracts from *The Life of Saint Teresa of Avila by Herself* translated by J.M.Cohen (Penguin Classics, 1957) copyright © J.M.Cohen, 1957.

Random House UK Ltd, 20 Vauxhall Bridge Road, London SW1V 2SA for the extract from *An Evil Cradling* by Brian Keenan, published by Hutchinson, London 1993.

St Vladimir Seminary Press, 575 Scarsdale Road, Crestwood, NY 10707, USA, for the extract from *On the Song of Songs, Sermones in Cantica Canticorum*, translated and edited by a Religious of C.S.M.V. (Mowbray, 1952).

A.P.Watt Ltd, 20 John Street, London WC1N 2DR on behalf of The Trustees of the Robert Graves Copyright Trust, for 'The Suicide in the Copse', taken from *Collected Poems* 1975 by Robert Graves.